USING A LAWYER

...And What to Do If Things Go Wrong

A STEP-BY-STEP GUIDE

A RANDOM HOUSE PRACTICAL LAW MANUAL

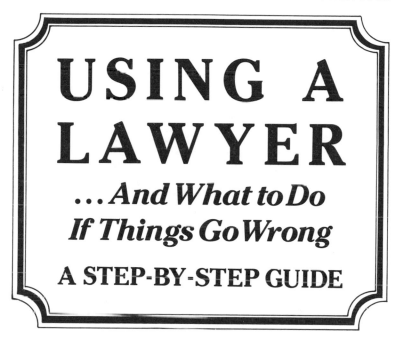

USING A LAWYER

...And What to Do If Things Go Wrong

A STEP-BY-STEP GUIDE

KAY OSTBERG
in Association with HALT

RANDOM HOUSE NEW YORK

HALT—An Organization of Americans for Legal Reform, is a national, nonprofit, nonpartisan public interest group with more than 150,000 members. Based in Washington, D.C., its goals are to enable people to handle their legal affairs simply, affordably, and equitably. HALT's education and advocacy programs strive to improve the quality, reduce the costs and increase the accessibility of the civil justice system. Its activities are funded by members' contributions.

The original draft of this book was coauthored by Adrien Helm. Substantial assistance with this book was provided by George Milko, Theresa Meehan Rudy and Richard Hébert

Library of Congress Cataloging-in-Publication Data

Ostberg, Kay.
    Using a lawyer . . . and what to do if things go wrong: a step-by-step guide/Kay Ostberg in association with HALT.
        p.   cm.—(A Random House practical law manual)
    First ed. written by Adrian Helm and Kay Ostberg. 1985.
    Includes bibliographical references.
    ISBN 0-679-72970-4
    1. Attorney and client—United States—Popular works. 2. Lawyers—United States—Fees—Popular works. I. Helm, Adrien. Using a lawyer . . . and what to do if things go wrong. II. HALT, Inc. III. Title. IV. Series.
    KF311.Z9H45   1990
    344.73′0176134—dc20   89-49427
    [347.304176134]   CIP

Book design by Charlotte Staub

Manufactured in the United States of America
Revised Edition

Contents

INTRODUCTION

This book is a consumer guide for managing your business dealings with a lawyer. It provides practical advice about how to avoid problems with the lawyers you hire and how to fire or bring action against them if preventive steps fail.

Lawyers sell legal services. As a customer, you choose the service you want to buy and come to an agreement on the terms of the purchase. You are the employer. It is your money, your property and your rights that are at stake. It is your responsibility to choose a lawyer carefully, to keep yourself informed about your case and to bring any problems to a lawyer's attention as soon as they arise. As with any purchase, you have the right to expect value for your dollar and to hold the seller to the terms of the purchase contract. This book will help you do that with information ranging from the general—explaining the business nature of the relationship—to the detailed—suggesting how to maintain control over your records.

It is organized chronologically, beginning with a discussion of alternative levels of client involvement and moving on to advice on shopping for a legal service plan or a lawyer. The book ends with strategies for redress if you have been a victim of attorney misconduct or if other problems occur with your attorney. Suggestions for effective resolution short of formal grievance proceedings are discussed. If these fail, formal remedies are explored, including official grievance procedures, arbitrating fee disputes, client security trust funds and malpractice suits. Guidelines are given to help you understand each of these processes.

Appendix I suggests a model client-attorney agreement; Appendix II translates a standard prepaid legal contract into plain language; Appendix III shows the procedural stages of a typical civil suit; Appendix IV contains state-by-state information about grievance, arbitration and client security fund mechanisms; Appendix V includes a glossary of basic terms used in the text or for procedures of a typical civil suit; and Appendix VI lists books on other topics including lawyer shopping directories.

A WORD ABOUT TERMS

Using A Lawyer uses common, everyday language. Where familiarity with a legal term can be helpful, the legal word or phrase is also included. The more acquainted you are with these few terms, the more confidently you will be able to negotiate the arrangements you want.

Appendix V includes a glossary of basic terms for procedures of a typical civil suit as well as terms used in the text. Familiarity with them will help you understand your case proceedings.

HOW TO USE THIS BOOK

It's best if you read the entire text through before hiring an attorney. That will give you a solid foundation upon which to build your client-attorney relationship.

If you already have a working relationship with a lawyer,

this book can still help you identify potential trouble spots. As we will explain, when trouble occurs, you should always act to modify the relationship. If nothing else, you can inform yourself about your legal concern, ask your lawyer or a second lawyer appropriate questions and become more actively involved in your case.

If you first pick up this book after you have developed problems with your lawyer, turn to the chapters that explain strategies for solving them. These chapters cover the most frequent types of client complaints, the pros and cons of firing an attorney and how to lodge a formal complaint against an attorney. They also tell you what to consider if you want to sue a lawyer for malpractice. In sum, the early chapters of the book can be compared to preventive medicine, the latter to medical treatment or surgery.

USING A LAWYER

...And What to Do If Things Go Wrong

A STEP-BY-STEP GUIDE

CHAPTER 1

CLIENT INVOLVEMENT

Clients who are fully informed are better equipped to make key decisions in their case, to avoid problems by spotting and solving them early on, and to monitor their attorney's actions.

Consumers hire attorneys for two things: their expertise in legal procedures and their familiarity with local courts and court personnel. You don't want your involvement to hinder your attorney from using the expertise you purchased, but you have no choice in the matter: you are involved. You are legally responsible for any actions your attorney takes in your name. The degree of active involvement you seek will affect the time and money you spend on a case and also how well you are informed about actions taken.

As a client, you can be involved at any of several different levels. You can handle your case on your own and use a lawyer only to review your paperwork, or you can use a lawyer in a more conventional way, hiring one to handle the entire case and give you progress reports. Between these two extremes are several other options. To determine which is most appropriate for you, you should educate yourself as much as you can about your case.

Begin with a book that discusses your kind of legal problem. There are plain-language books available on legal topics ranging from fighting traffic tickets to do-it-yourself divorces.

Check with HALT and your local bookstores and public libraries for written resources prepared for nonlawyers. A law library can provide further education.

You should also be familiar with court procedures and the stages of a typical lawsuit. Appendix III of this book guides you through these stages and defines the terms used. Knowing these steps and the legal terms involved will make it easier for you to work with your lawyer. Bear in mind, however, that not every case involves all the stages of our model; don't feel something is wrong simply because some steps are omitted. In fact, most cases are settled out of court and never reach the trial stage.

You can also try to get information by talking to clerks at the courthouse or to the staff of a government agency, legal aid office or law school clinic. These people are familiar with court procedures, and they are used to dealing with nonlawyers. But don't be surprised if court clerks resist giving you information because they are afraid of violating rules against nonlawyers' giving legal advice. And don't be surprised if other members of the staff are too busy to talk with you.

Educating yourself about your case will help you answer four basic questions:

- How can using the legal system solve your problem?
- Do you want to handle the case on your own using self-help materials?
- Do you want to use mediation or some other alternative to litigation to solve your problem?
- Do you want to hire an attorney?

DECIDE ON YOUR LAWYER'S ROLE

If you do decide to hire an attorney, you can hire one as a *pro se* coach. This means that you would be on record as representing yourself and would do the actual work on your case. The attorney would be paid an hourly fee to review your work or to coach you before a hearing or other court proceeding. If, for example, you own a small apartment building, you might know enough to take your own cases into court to enforce leases or collect bills but want to hire an attorney to coach you on recent changes in the law or to review your court papers for accuracy.

If you decide to have an attorney do most of the work, you can still do work on the case that will save the lawyer's time and your money. You can volunteer to undertake tasks essential to your case that don't require a lawyer's specialized training. For example, you can run errands to get forms, search public records, research government regulations or compile data to support your case—data you are probably more familiar with than your attorney is. These are only a few of the kinds of practical support you can give your lawyer. Propose money-saving alternatives whenever they occur to you, and ask the lawyer to suggest chores you can do to speed the case and lower your costs.

Legal problems aren't like broken pipes. You don't simply call a lawyer and say "fix it" unless you don't care how it is fixed or how much the repair costs. You hire an attorney because you want legal expertise, but you imperil your pocketbook and the outcome of your case if you adopt an attitude of "send me the bill." Whatever degree of involvement you decide on, it is essential to communicate to your attorney both your willingness and your intention to be helpful and your ownership of the legal matter under consideration. If the relationship works right, you and your lawyer are partners working for a common goal—with you as the senior partner.

CHAPTER 2

LEGAL SERVICE PLANS

This chapter discusses shopping for a legal service plan. Most people hire a lawyer to handle a specific legal task rather than enrolling in a plan. However, you may find your legal needs would be met by joining such a plan instead of hiring a lawyer. This chapter explains how legal service plans operate, the different types available and the limitations of such plans.

Legal service plans started as an employer-paid group benefit for union members. More recently, they have become available to other kinds of groups and private individuals, with forty-five million people participating. How successful legal service plans will be is still speculative, because they are relatively new.

Most people participate in legal service plans through their unions, associations or employers. Such group legal service plans are usually not available to the public. Individual or private plans are offered directly to the public through direct mail, telemarketing and door-to-door sales. Ordinarily, anyone can join an individual plan. The exceptions are plans sold solely to the members of a specific credit card company or credit union. Because these individual plans involve payment of an annual or monthly fee before legal services can be rendered, they are called prepaid.

Prepaid legal plans offer members limited services for a

flat yearly or monthly fee. Besides giving ready access to lawyers at lower-than-normal rates for basic legal advice, they eliminate the time clients have to spend "shopping" for a lawyer. Under most plans, lawyers have been preselected for them.

Like health maintenance organizations (HMOs), prepaid legal plans rely on the economy of spreading the risk among a large group of people with the expectation that only a few will take advantage of the benefits. They also mirror HMOs in their emphasis on "preventive law."

Legal service plans allow groups of people to pool their purchasing power to get legal services free or at reduced prices. However, not everyone needs to belong to a plan. You should evaluate your legal needs carefully before joining a plan and then, if you want to join, shop carefully for the plan that best meets those needs.

INDIVIDUAL VERSUS GROUP PLANS

Individual plans usually have a higher per-member operating cost than do group plans because they don't have the economic advantage of drawing on a large pool of available participants.

In group plans, the sponsor (employer, union or association) may pay all or part of the membership fees. In individual plans, each member is responsible for the entire annual or monthly fee.

A group plan may or may not be prepaid. If no advance fee is required of the group or its members, it is "free." The largest "free" group legal plan, called Union Privilege Legal Services, is offered by the AFL-CIO. It is subscribed to by forty-nine of its labor unions, with over ten million members.

In an individual prepaid legal service plan, an annual or monthly fee is paid in advance in exchange for advice from a lawyer and other specified routine legal help. The fee (normally referred to as the membership or enrollment fee) is paid either by the sponsoring group or by individual members. If the sponsoring group pays the fee, its members are considered to be automatically enrolled. If members pay, membership begins only after the fee is paid.

Whether it's a group or private plan, a plan administrator is responsible for promoting the plan, handling its finances, enrolling members and paying the fees owed to participating lawyers.

GOVERNMENT REGULATION

Some states regulate plans like insurance, while others have statutes that give special jurisdiction to the insurance commissioner but treat the plans as special entities not modeled on insurance. At least twenty-five states have specific legislation that governs the way these plans can operate in order to ensure that members get what they pay for.

Insurance commissioners are often entrusted with this job because many of these plans look and operate like insurance—you pay now and get the services later. To obtain information about how a particular plan is regulated in your state, contact your state's insurance commissioner, listed in the telephone book under your state government offices.

WHAT PLANS OFFER

Most plans encourage "preventive law" by urging their members to get in touch with lawyers early and to use them as advisors. The result is that legal opinions are sought on subjects not normally referred to lawyers because of the expense involved. The medical saying "An ounce of prevention is worth a pound of cure" is applied by these plans to your legal well-being as well on the theory that early information can prevent the need for more expensive legal help down the line.

The type, size, coverage and cost of these plans vary widely. Under some, the coverage changes depending on the state you live in. However, most plans, whether group or individual, offer the following: help in selecting a lawyer, unlimited legal counseling, telephone and letter follow-ups, will drafting, document review and reduced rates for legal matters that go beyond what's offered for the annual membership fee. Some plans also offer litigation services.

Help in Selecting Lawyers. Under most plans, the administrator decides which lawyer will be assigned to your legal matter. A few plans allow you either to select your own lawyer or to select from a panel of lawyers. The advantage of getting a single lawyer or group of lawyers to choose from is that you don't have to spend time "shopping." The disadvantage is that you lose control and freedom to choose whom you'll work with.

We suggest that when you evaluate plans, be sure to ask if you will be allowed to switch lawyers if the one appointed for you or whom you choose from a list turns out to be unsatisfactory. Find out how difficult this is to do. Is the plan receptive to such requests, or will you be forced to wait a long while because you want a different lawyer?

Ask also if you'll be given advance information about the plan's participating lawyers. Typically, such information is only given to members who ask for it. Try to find out how long the plan lawyers have been in practice, in what areas of law they practice and whether they carry malpractice insurance. Plan lawyers have generally been in practice at least five years and are usually required by plan administrators to carry malpractice insurance.

Unlimited Telephone Counseling. Most plans offer unlimited telephone consultation, as long as each call is about a new matter. In other words, you can pick up the telephone during normal working hours and get a lawyer at the other end without worrying about the cost. There's no limit on the amount of time you spend talking. However, you cannot keep calling back about the same problem. Members use this service to get quick advice about such things as resolving a problem with a neighbor or business or service professional or dealing with traffic violations, simple estate planning questions or housing or rental agreements.

You may not always get to speak to the same lawyer. If you like the idea of developing a continuing working relationship with one lawyer, ask if that can be accommodated by the plan you're considering.

Office Visits.   Under most plans, for any new legal problem, you also have the option of an in-person visit, usually limited to one hour or less.

If you want to meet with the lawyer more than once on the same legal matter, you will be charged at the plan's rate, which can vary from $50 to $100 an hour. Incurring such additional expenses can be avoided, however, if you can resolve legal matters over the telephone or by asking the lawyer to make a call or write a letter on your behalf.

Follow-ups.   Follow-up correspondence by either telephone or letter is included under most plans. Some plans allow their lawyers to handle an unlimited number of calls or free letters on your behalf, but others limit such follow-up work. For example, a lawyer may be able to make only one call or write one letter on your behalf per problem per year of membership. If you think you will require a lot of lawyer intervention (for example, to deal with ongoing business or unruly-neighbor problems), you'll want a plan that doesn't restrict the amount of follow-up help a lawyer can give you.

Documents.   For your membership fee, most plans also offer simple will drafting and review of legal documents such as rental agreements, incorporation papers or repair contracts. A few plans offer more, including documents such as deeds or powers of attorney.

If document drafting is your major reason for joining, a plan may be a good idea. After all, even simple wills can cost as much as $200 in some parts of the country, and with a legal service plan you can have both the will and other benefits for less than that. Be careful, however, when shopping for a plan. Find out what's meant by a "simple will" and whether it will take care of your full estate-planning needs. For example, does a simple will include drawing up a minor's trust? How many beneficiaries can be named? Does the plan charge extra if you need to make changes down the line? Some plans include changes (codicils) at no extra charge. Will the plan charge extra for your spouse's will?

Find out if the plan limits the number and length of legal documents you can submit for free review each year. Most plans don't limit the number but do limit the number of pages each document can have—usually fewer than ten. Some plans also refuse to review documents that don't have your name on them.

Reduced Rates. Some plans offer guaranteed prices on more complex legal matters such as complex estate planning, real estate transactions, adoptions and divorces. This can be either a saving or a money drain in disguise. Check prices with lawyers outside the plan to make sure you're getting the best deal and the most suitable lawyer for your task. You might also consider handling some legal matters on your own to keep legal costs down. For example, a plan may offer name changes for $155—which sounds reasonable, but only until you learn you can easily change your name on your own by going down to the courthouse and filing a piece of paper for a nominal filing fee.

Litigation Services. Don't expect legal service plans to handle any litigation without charge. Most plans do not provide representation in court for the basic membership fee, and of those that do, most exclude criminal cases, services for which a percentage fee is generally charged (such as personal injury suits) and appeals. Some plans provide lawyer representation for members when they are being sued, but not for members who file lawsuits against someone else.

Most plans do, however, provide free advice about litigation and will appoint a lawyer to represent you in litigation at reduced hourly rates.

Other Considerations. Ask where the plan is available and whether you can still get coverage if you move or travel out of state. For example, will the plan accommodate your needs if you live in Ohio but get into trouble with an auto repair shop or traffic court in Michigan?

By making access easier and less expensive, plans encourage people who have legal questions or problems to consult lawyers more often, but you should be careful of becoming too dependent on lawyers. Instead of meeting the plans' objective of lowering legal expenses, such dependency could end up increasing your legal costs.

TYPES OF PLANS

There are two basic categories of legal service plans—access and comprehensive.

• *Access plans.* Offered to the general public, access plans concentrate on giving members easy access to lawyers for routine legal services. They typically provide free and often unlimited telephone consultations with lawyers, a review of legal documents up to six or seven pages long and preparation of a simple will. For more complex legal matters, members are referred to a panel of participating lawyers who agree to perform legal services at discounted prices.

• *Comprehensive plans.* As their name implies, these cover every legal need you have. They are offered only to groups, not to individuals. Typically, an employer sponsors a comprehensive plan as a benefit to employees, who participate without cost.

Comprehensive plans give the same benefits as access plans and then some. For example, at no additional cost to the employee, lawyers will draft any legal document and provide legal representation in or out of court. The plans even reimburse their members for legal expenses or fees they incur (for example, defending against traffic citations).

Open and Closed Panels. Plans deliver legal services to their members through one of two arrangements: closed panels or open panels. Premiums for open-panel systems are generally higher than for closed-panel systems because they give you more choices among lawyers.

Most plans operate closed panels, whereby the plan manager either hires a group of lawyers to work for plan members or contracts with a law firm to do all the work. Closed plans generally offer you a greater variety of legal services and lower premiums.

One disadvantage is that members have little or no voice in choosing which lawyers do their legal work. Some closed plans assign you to a specific lawyer; others allow you to choose from a limited list. Because legal advice is only as good as the lawyer giving it, it's important to find out if you can dismiss an unsatisfactory lawyer and select or be appointed to another.

Open-panel plans allow you to choose a lawyer from a list that is larger than closed-plan lists. The lawyer agrees to a schedule of fixed fees for the services offered. Under this system, each lawyer is paid only for the work performed. Each lawyer is paid by the plan as the specific work is done, much as doctors are paid by health insurance companies. In open-panel systems, while you have greater freedom of choice, lawyers are not guaranteed a particular amount of legal business from the plan and therefore have little incentive to take business from plan members and charge below their normal rates.

SHOPPING FOR A PLAN

Before choosing a legal service plan, evaluate your needs and decide what type of plan will best meet them. Here are four more important rules to follow:

1. If you have a legal problem that needs immediate attention, spend your time and energy looking for appropriate help, not shopping for a plan. Even though you may find a plan that assigns you to a lawyer immediately, you're leaving it to chance that you'll be referred to the best lawyer for the problem at hand. It makes more sense to shop for a legal service plan when you have time and aren't influenced by specific pressing concerns.
2. Send for information on all available plans. The National Resource Center for Consumers of Legal Services can send you a list of the major ones and their addresses. Simply send a stamped, self-addressed envelope to them at: 1444 I St. NW, 8th Fl., Washington, D.C. 20005.
3. Don't be swayed by the typical high-pressure sales talk used in direct mail. Don't be pressured into signing before you're ready. These plans need many members to successfully continue offering low membership rates. Don't worry, your money will be accepted when you're ready to give it.

4. Learn all you can about the history and operation of the organization that's running the program to be sure it's reputable. Plan representatives should be willing to answer your questions. Some specific ones to ask:

- How long has the program been in operation? (New plans have yet to demonstrate a track record or develop a full array of smoothly operating services.)
- How many lawyers participate in the plan? Has the number increased or decreased during the past year? (A growing plan is healthier and more likely to meet your future needs.)
- Are panels open or closed?
- Can you switch lawyers if you're unhappy with the one appointed to you? (If not, watch out.)
- How big is the plan? How many people have enrolled?
- Does it include a grievance or complaint system?
- Does it allow you to evaluate services annually and drop your membership if you're unsatisfied?
- What happens if the plan goes out of business? Do you get a refund?
- What references can the plan furnish?

The contract to join an individual legal service plan is a simple form that briefly describes the agreement and refers you to a brochure for more details about the terms and benefits of membership. The form simply requires your signature and, if you're not paying by check, a credit card number. A plain-language explanation of a typical plan can be found in Appendix II.

The information you need to know about the plan is covered not in the agreement form but in the brochure. Most such brochures are written in plain language with a lot of sales talk. These promotional brochures list both the free benefits you get by joining the plan and the benefits that are available at reduced rates.

CHAPTER 3

SHOPPING FOR A LAWYER

This chapter discusses the major techniques you can use in shopping for and choosing a lawyer if you are not a member of a legal service plan. Careful shopping is important; it is your first and best opportunity to make sure you are hiring a lawyer in whom you have confidence and with whom you will be able to work. Comparative shopping for a lawyer helps you:

- Understand the range of services and prices available
- Compare differing views on your legal problem
- Select a lawyer who is likely to handle your case as you expect

LIST YOUR PROSPECTS

Your first step in hiring an attorney is to generate a list of prospects. Ask for recommendations from business acquaintances, relatives, friends, and professionals such as clergy, counselors, social workers and physicians. The foundation of a good lawyer-client relationship is mutual respect, so you should solicit suggestions from people whose judgment you consider sound.

It is not enough to get an endorsement like "So-and-so is a fine lawyer." You need specific information about the kinds of problems the lawyer has handled and why the person is recommending this particular one. This will enable you to evaluate the recommendation in light of your problem and how you want to handle it.

You can also get names of attorneys from groups that work on issues related to your legal concern. These may be private organizations, government agencies, local bar associations, legal aid organizations or public interest groups. For example, you might want to ask the National Organization for Women's Legal Defense and Education Fund for referrals to lawyers who specialize in sex discrimination cases or HALT for lawyers who specialize in legal malpractice cases. In particular, local service organizations often maintain lists of attorneys willing to accept referrals. Attorneys agree to be listed with them because they are interested in a particular area of the law, because they are public-spirited, and because they want to generate business.

Law schools and private legal clinics are other sources of lawyer prospects. Many law schools operate legal clinics to give their students "real world" experience on legal cases under the supervision of attorneys. Most of these clinics serve clients with limited incomes and charge no fees. However, some law school clinics specialize by subject area, such as small-business law or antidiscrimination cases, and serve clients regardless of their income.

Private legal clinics are staffed by lawyers who handle large numbers of routine legal matters, such as will drafting, lease writing, uncontested divorces and bankruptcy. By accepting a large volume of similar types of cases, these clinics are able to keep costs down and charge clients lower fees than most private law firms can. Be as careful in selecting a lawyer in a legal clinic as you would be in selecting any lawyer. Find out how long the clinic has been in business and talk to others who have used the clinic's services. Ask the clinic's lawyer the questions that appear on page 21.

You can find the names of lawyers in the yellow pages and various directories that can be found in law libraries. The bibliography in Appendix VI includes lawyer shopping directories. One directory, the *Martindale-Hubbell Law Directory,* is a well-known "Who's Who" of lawyers with brief biographical information provided by the lawyers themselves and a rating system. The ratings are of limited help, however, because they are based on opinions of fellow lawyers, not clients. Be careful to assess the information in any directory by finding out first who put the information together and why.

Your search has just begun when you have compiled a list of names. You should use this list the way you would use a page of want ads for used cars. It is now time to contact the prospects you've identified and begin to judge the quality of the services they offer.

INITIAL CONTACT

Telephone each prospect. This initial contact will help you shorten your list. Prepare for the calls by writing down the questions you want to ask each lawyer. If you are well organized and know what you want to ask and how you want to ask it, you will save time for both yourself and the attorney and demonstrate your intention and ability to remain in charge of your legal affairs in a businesslike, professional way.

Use the telephone call to:

1. Identify yourself and explain that you are hiring an attorney to help you with a case involving _____.
2. Determine the cost, if any, of an initial consultation interview.

3. Ask any questions you think are important and that can be answered by yes, no or other brief answers. For example, you can ask:
   - Have you handled this kind of case before?
   - Do you sign written fee agreements with clients?
   - What are your usual rates for this type of case?
   - Are your fees negotiable?
   - How many years have you practiced?
   - Can you refer me to clients for whom you've handled cases like mine?
   - Do you represent any client groups, such as senior citizens?
   - Do you carry malpractice insurance?

4. Answer any questions the attorney may have.
5. Ask about problems that may arise while the attorney is working on your case.
6. Schedule an in-person interview if the prospect still appears worth pursuing.

You can discover much from this sort of initial contact. If, for example, you are not allowed to talk with the lawyer who will be working on your case, this tells you something about how the office is run. The senior attorney may be the salesperson who is prepared for your questions. The junior attorney who will handle your case could be less experienced. If it is clear that the lawyer is unhappy that you want to conduct an interview before hiring, this lawyer may not be for you.

Before attending an interview, contact your state disciplinary agency (see Appendix IV) to find out if the lawyer you are considering interviewing has ever been publicly disciplined. You can also make sure that the lawyer is licensed to practice law in your state.

Don't feel bad if, after making several calls, you call back to cancel some appointments. Conducting more than three or four interviews will be time-consuming and probably unnecessary, so don't be shy about selecting only your prime candidates to interview.

THE INTERVIEW

The interview is for finding out as much as you can about the lawyer. It is *not* the time to tell the attorney everything there is to know about your legal concern. Give enough information so the lawyer can accurately explain how your problem would be handled. You have three goals in this interview:

- To determine if the lawyer is experienced, able and willing to undertake your case
- To understand what services will be performed for you and how much you will be charged for them
- To learn whether you will be comfortable working with the lawyer

Prepare for the interview by writing a brief summary of your case, including all relevant dates and all major facts. The lawyer will need some of this information immediately, and you will save time if it is prepared for presentation. Prepare a list of questions to ask the lawyers you interview. During the interview, make notes of the lawyer's answers so you can compare them when making your final choice.

Any questions you feel comfortable asking and that will elicit information pertinent to your goals will do, but don't wander too far afield from your primary objective, evaluating the lawyer's ability to handle your case. One further warning: don't be so preoccupied with your "script" of questions that you forget to listen to the answers for both content and style.

In addition to asking any questions not answered in your initial telephone call, you might ask the lawyer the following:
- What will be the likely result of my suit? (This could take the form of: How much can I win? What might I lose? What is the other side likely to settle for? What do you think a court would award?)
- What are my legal options and what option do you recommend? Do you think the case would go to litigation or be settled out of court?
- How long will this matter take to complete?
- How do you calculate legal fees? How much are the legal fees likely to total?
- Will I have to pay a deposit (retainer)? How much will it be?
- How much will I pay in legal expenses?
- Describe your experience with cases such as mine.
- Do you have a standard legal service agreement? If not, would you be willing to sign such an agreement?
- How do you resolve disputes with your clients? Would you be willing to use mediation to resolve any dispute?

It cannot be overemphasized that you are establishing a relationship that cannot work if you and the lawyer do not respect one another. Approach the interview seriously. Be businesslike, listen carefully and communicate accurately and with interest.

Chapters 4 and 5 of this book cover employment and fee agreements. These are critical to discuss in your interview, because misunderstandings most often occur between lawyers and clients over expectations about services and fees that weren't clearly specified at the outset. The questions you ask in this area should give you a clear understanding of the lawyer's standard practice. Remember, at this point you have not decided to hire this lawyer.

MAKING A DECISION

Immediately after each interview, review your notes to make sure they accurately reflect the exchange that occurred. Your notes will be helpful when it's time to make your choice. When all interviews are completed, balance each lawyer's strengths and weaknesses, deciding which factors are most important to you and whether you have a clear choice.

For example, a lawyer newly admitted to the bar may be less expensive and quite capable of reviewing your simple will, but if you want help in preparing a complex estate plan complete with several trusts, you probably want a seasoned tax and estate-planning specialist. If you are suing a local lawyer, the most important factor may be to hire an out-of-town attorney, even though it means you will have to pay the lawyer's travel expenses.[1]

If none of the lawyers you interview meets your needs, look for other prospects by drawing up a new list or going back to your old list and calling others to schedule interviews. Unless you are under extreme pressure to resolve your case quickly, it is far better to invest additional time at this stage than to try to undo a poor decision later.

Once you have made your choice, call the attorney and make an appointment to discuss employment and fee agreements, the subject of the next two chapters.

---

[1] *Directory of Lawyers Who Sue Lawyers,* Kay Ostberg and George Milko in association with HALT, 1989. Available from HALT.

CHAPTER 4

FEE ARRANGEMENTS

An employment agreement is a legally binding contract enforceable in court. It spells out the terms of your relationship with your lawyer and the fees you can be charged. (The terms "agreement" and "contract" are used interchangeably in this book.) If you don't have a written agreement, you will have no way to prove the terms you negotiated. It will be your word against that of your lawyer.

Some attorneys don't tell their clients before taking a case how they calculate their fees or what expenses a client can expect to pay in addition to fees. Others fail to document hours and expenses when they bill clients. Written fee agreements can prevent these problems, but such agreements are voluntary. It is up to you, the client, to make sure you have one with your lawyer, and that you get it in writing. The fact that fee disputes are the most common attorney-client problem should convince you of the benefits of written agreements. They can prevent misunderstandings, surprise expenses and overcharging.

An employment agreement should cover two things: fees and the terms of employment. This chapter discusses how fees are assessed, what services are covered and what is "extra." Chapter 5 covers the other terms of employment, including:

- *Retainers*—the amount you have to pay, how it will be used and whether it is refundable
- *Expenses*—an estimate of the costs and how they are to be paid
- *Billings*—how often itemized bills will be sent to you and when payments are due
- *Timetable*—an estimate of the total time the case will take and when each stage of work will be complete
- *Conflict resolution*—how disputes will be resolved, procedures for modifying the agreement and procedures to follow if you decide to terminate the lawyer-client relationship
- *Responsibilities*—what the lawyer and you are each responsible for doing

If the attorney you want to hire refuses to agree to a contract, it may be time to reconsider your choice. It cannot be overemphasized how important this agreement might be to you. In particular:
- It can prevent misunderstandings. ("I didn't know the expenses would be deducted *after* the attorney's third was taken out!")
- It can provide a measure of the attorney's conduct. ("I thought all attorneys billed at the *end* of the case, not every month!")
- It gives you written proof of your understanding.
- The attorney is aware that you will use the agreement to measure case progress and thus is more likely to abide by the terms of the agreement.

THE "REASONABLE" FEE

In the absence of a fee agreement to the contrary, the law allows an attorney to collect a "reasonable" fee. The definition of "reasonable" fee varies from state to state, but one of the factors often considered is the dollar value of the transaction involved. An attorney who has not signed a contract or who has included a vague, catchall clause in your contract can often claim a percentage of the settlement as a fee. Thus the fee may be based not only on the time spent or the difficulty of the work done but on what the financial settlement is.

THREE KINDS OF FEES

It is important to understand the three main kinds of fees that lawyers charge and the incentives lawyers have for using each. Remember, it is up to you to negotiate the fee structure that suits you best. Few laws govern lawyers' fees. Those that do usually involve little more than setting a fee ceiling for certain types of cases. For example, a lawyer in New York can charge a maximum of 25% of the amount awarded in Social Security cases. In the absence of such laws, fee agreements are the consumer's only protection against excessive "reasonable" fees.

Hourly Fees

Hourly fees are based on the number of hours worked. If your lawyer charges $100 an hour, your fee will be $100 multiplied by the number of hours worked. Lawyers also bill for partial hours spent, usually by the quarter or tenth of an hour. For example, if your $100-an-hour lawyer charges in quarter-hour increments, expect to be billed $25 for a five-minute telephone call.

Under an hourly-fee arrangement, the more hours worked, the bigger the bill. This rewards the lawyer who puts in more hours on your case, whether or not it needs that much time, and serves as an incentive to prolong cases rather than to bring them to a quick conclusion. This may not be in the client's best interest.

You can prevent "overlawyering" by comparing your bills to the estimates you collected on the number of hours your case would take, including the estimate in your agreement. By checking your itemized bills, you can determine at each stage whether or not your lawyer is exceeding the hours expected. Whenever you suspect "overlawyering," discuss it with your attorney.

If you agree to an hourly rate, you don't want to pay the attorney's hourly fee for typing done by a secretary, for a messenger delivering your documents across town, or for a law clerk looking up the laws involved in your case. Make sure that you know, and that your agreement specifies, the hourly rates you'll pay for support staff work.

Hourly rates are usually preferable to contingency fee arrangements because they are based on the time the attorney spends working on your case. However, you must watch for the attorney who is learning the law on your money and the one who sees your case as an opportunity to prolong a suit and bill you accordingly.

Flat Fees

Legal clinics and many lawyers now offer flat fees for routine legal matters, such as will preparation, incorporation of a business, lease preparation, some probate work, uncontested divorces and other uncomplicated matters. A flat fee means you will be charged a specified total for work on your case. For example, a lawyer might offer to prepare your will for $100, regardless of how long it takes. Often an agreement with a flat fee will require that the client also pay such "extras" as filing fees, photocopying and other out-of-pocket or unanticipated expenses.

Flat fees are charged when lawyers can accurately predict the average amount of time a case will take. Such work usually can be completed by filling out standard forms or is almost identical to numerous other cases handled by the office. Recognize, however, that a flat fee reflects an hourly rate, so ask how much time the work will take, include this estimate in your agreement and choose an hourly figure if the math is in your favor. Usually, however, flat fees turn out to be bargains because when the work is repetitive and time-saving forms are used, the savings are passed on to the clients.

A fixed maximum fee is similar to the flat fee. Under this plan you will be charged hourly; the total fee can be less but not greater than the fixed maximum. Any fixed maximum should be explained in your agreement.

Flat fees allow you to shop around among lawyers if you have a routine matter. Ask what specifics the flat fee covers in each case to be sure the various attorneys are offering the same services for the quoted price. In other words, if one lawyer's flat fee includes typing and copying costs and another's identical fee does not, the first lawyer is more economical. If you agree to a flat fee, make sure your agreement specifies exactly what the fee covers as well as any costs that are not included.

Contingency Fees

Contingency fees are most common in personal injury or collection cases in which the client cannot afford to pay if the case is lost. If you win, your lawyer gets a percentage of the winnings; if you lose, the lawyer doesn't get paid. The theory behind contingency fees is simple: the attorney takes the risk of losing; the greater the risk, the bigger the percentage.

If you win, the attorney often reaps a windfall on the theory that the attorney must also absorb a loss on the contingency fee cases that didn't succeed. However, what usually happens is that lawyers rarely accept cases in which much, if any, risk is involved. Contingency fees are popular among lawyers in this country but are illegal in Canada, India and most of Europe.

The customary contingency fee is 33% of the settlement, although fees range from 15% to 50%. Some lawyers offer a sliding scale in which the percentage changes depending on the stage at which the case is settled. For example, the lawyer may collect 25% if you settle before trial, 30% if there is a trial and 40% if there is an appeal.

Although a sliding scale might seem attractive at first glance, be wary. If you agree to a sliding scale, your attorney may try to get you to accept settlement because going to trial involves more time and work, even though you would do better to continue pursuing the case. Also recognize that when you weigh a settlement offer, you will have to consider paying an additional 5% in attorney fees if you reject it and go to trial. So if you accept a sliding scale geared to settlement, keep in mind that your interest and that of your attorney may not be the same as the case develops.

If a contingency fee arrangement is the only option available to you, follow these tips:

1. Find out how much the other person or the insurance company will offer you directly, without the help of an attorney.
2. Ask several lawyers to estimate your chances of success, how much you might be awarded and how many hours the case will take. Be suspicious of estimates that vary widely from others you've received. Ask the attorney if the fees are negotiable.
3. Using the estimates, calculate how much you can expect to receive after paying attorney fees and expenses. If it is about the same as what was offered you directly, negotiate a settlement on your own.
4. If you decide to hire a lawyer, figure out the approximate hourly rate, based on your estimates. If the probable con-

tingency fee is substantially higher than the lawyer's regular hourly rate, bargain for one of these alternatives:
- A set hourly rate; this is particularly appropriate if you are sure of winning or you want the lawyer to serve as a consultant rather than handle the entire case
- An hourly rate with an additional percentage amount if the lawyer wins substantially more than you were offered
- A sliding scale based on the amount of the award—for example, 33% for the first $5,000, 25% for the next $5,000 and so on

5. Ask that the percentage fee be calculated after expenses have been subtracted from the award. This can result in substantial savings. Consider the following example:

CONTINGENCY FEE FIRST		EXPENSES FIRST	
Total award	$90,000	Total award	$90,000
Lawyer fee (⅓)	−$30,000	Less expenses	−$12,000
Remainder	$60,000	Remainder	$78,000
Less expenses	−$12,000	Lawyer fee	−$26,000
Net to You:	$48,000	Net to You:	$52,000

6. Set a limit on the amount of expenses you can be billed for. If more expense money is needed, make sure your agreement requires your lawyer to get your express approval.

CHAPTER 5

TERMS OF EMPLOYMENT

In addition to negotiating how your lawyer is going to calculate the fee, you must also negotiate the other terms of the client-lawyer relationship—whether you will have to pay a retainer, what expenses you will have to pay, when and how you will be billed, how much time the case will take, what the progress reports will include so you can monitor developments, how conflicts between you and the lawyer will be resolved, and, if they cannot be, how and under what circumstances you can fire your lawyer.

This chapter examines each of these employment contract provisions in turn and offers suggestions you may want to incorporate into your final agreement with your lawyer. In addition, Appendix I offers a model client-attorney contract you may want to use as a guide.

RETAINERS

The term "retainer" is often used imprecisely and can be a source of confusion, particularly as to whether it is refundable or not, which varies according to your agreement with the lawyer. If you agree to any type of retainer, be careful that your agreement specifies what is meant.

Pure Retainers
These are fees paid to law firms to assure that a particular lawyer or firm will do all the client's work over a fixed period

of time, typically a year. They are often used by businesses to secure the services of a particular lawyer or firm thought to be expert in a given field and to keep that lawyer or firm from representing competitors. Fees for work actually done are paid in addition to the retainer. The retainer generally is not refundable.

Case Retainers

These fees are paid to retain the services of an attorney at the beginning of a case. This is the kind of retainer most often paid by the typical legal consumer. It may represent all of the fee, none of the fee or a portion of it. It may be refunded or not, depending on your agreement.

For example, a lawyer may charge you a flat fee of $600 for an uncontested divorce and ask you to pay a retainer of one quarter—$150—up front. This money may also be used to pay expenses associated with the case, such as filing fees. The important thing to make clear at the outset is whether the retainer is an advance on expenses, fees or both, and whether any unused part of it will be refunded.

General Representation Retainers

These retainers are used to cover a predictable level of legal work needed on a regular basis. They give businesses ready access to legal advice and routine services. The retainers are billed periodically and make the law firm readily available for work by telephone, review of documents or other volume work. Usually such a retainer will not cover extraordinary legal projects like complex litigation and is not refundable.

EXPENSES

In addition to fees you will probably have to pay all the expenses or "costs" of your case. These can include court filing fees, fees for expert witnesses and money for transcripts, stenographers, copying, mailing, long distance telephone calls and transportation for out-of-town attorneys. If your case goes to trial, these expenses can be quite high.

You may be asked to pay an advance against costs at the time you hire your attorney. Any bill you receive should include an itemized list of expenses. Advances are intended to cover expenses that arise in the course of employment. As an advance, these fees should be refunded if not spent, but make sure that your agreement clearly specifies that they will be. Get a receipt so you will have a record of what has been advanced to compare against an itemized bill.

If you or your lawyer thinks the expenses in your case will be high, it is a good idea to set a limit on the amount you can be charged, based on your attorney's estimate. Then, if more needs to be set aside, your agreement can require your attorney to get your express approval.

Expert witnesses are particularly expensive, but often necessary in complex lawsuits. Make sure you understand what you are paying for and why your attorney wants to hire the expert. Understand that the expert will cost you not only for the time spent testifying at trial, but for trial preparation, pretrial questioning and travel. If you are told that the firm always uses a particular expert witness, ask about the firm's win-loss record using that expert's testimony and if there are less expensive alternatives.

BILLING ARRANGEMENTS

Billing arrangements should be spelled out in your agreement. Bills provide a history of your dealings with your lawyer and serve to spread payments out over a period of time. They also serve as a management tool for you because they remind the lawyer that you expect periodic progress reports on your case and want to know all steps taken on your behalf.

In most cases you should ask for monthly itemized bills. If you anticipate long periods of inaction on your case, you can modify this requirement. You should ask that the itemization reflect the time spent on your case, what was done and all expenses to date. Remember, support staff hours should be listed separately from the attorney's hours. The more detailed your bill, the better you will understand what is happening on your case and how much money you are spending on it.

Most attorneys are willing to allow clients to pay in installments. If you think you will need to spread your payments out over a longer period than it may to take to resolve your legal problem, ask the attorney about this. Any arrangement you come to should be written into your agreement.

TIMETABLE

Your agreement should estimate the total time the case will take and spell out the precise tasks the attorney will perform for you and how long they will take. The attorney may find the time difficult to predict, but even "ball park" estimates will be extremely valuable to you.

This timetable will allow you to judge the progress of your case. It should identify the logical stages of the case. These are likely to be the most convenient times for you to discuss with your lawyer such things as case progress and your degree of involvement in the process. If work is not proceeding on schedule, the timetable will reveal this and enable you to discuss it knowledgeably with the attorney to discover the reason and decide what, if anything, should be done about it.

RESOLVING DISPUTES

Remember the adage about "an ounce of prevention" when approaching the question of how you and your lawyer will resolve conflicts. It is important for you to have discussed what mechanisms you will use if problems arise during the course of the attorney's employment. It is a difficult subject because it is much like writing a separation agreement on the eve of a wedding, but writing the terms of conflict resolution into your agreement can save you both time and money later on.

You can include a clause specifying that you and your attorney will agree to discuss all causes of dissatisfaction openly and seek reconciliation. You should specify that there will be no fee charged for time spent trying to resolve this dissatisfaction. You can specify that if this informal method of resolution fails, you will resolve the difficulty through more formal mechanisms, such as mediation or arbitration.

For example, you may be completely satisfied with the quality of the work being done, but feel you are being unfairly billed. It is perfectly proper to include in your agreement a clause specifying that any fee disputes will be settled by mediation or arbitration. You can also agree that other disputes between you and the lawyer will be settled through these mechanisms. The important thing to remember is that the issue of conflicts must be directly addressed by your agreement.

ATTORNEY WITHDRAWAL OR FIRING

Chapter 8 of this book includes a full discussion of the pros and cons of firing your attorney and facts about attorney withdrawal. Here we are concerned only with the terms of firing or withdrawal that you may want to include in your agreement with your lawyer.

If your lawyer withdraws from your case before trial, it can cause you serious delay and cost considerable money to educate a new lawyer about your case. For that reason you might want to include in your agreement a provision that your lawyer cannot withdraw without fourteen days' notice or within thirty days of trial, except for extreme reasons such as illness, or death in the family. Include a provision that the attorney cannot withdraw if the withdrawal will significantly affect the outcome of imminent proceedings or if a competent lawyer cannot be found as a replacement. Stipulate that if the attorney wants to withdraw, the withdrawal must be in writing and include the reasons for the withdrawal. This can be important if you decide to file a grievance or pursue a malpractice action later on.

Recognize also that unless you provide otherwise in the agreement, when your lawyer withdraws or is fired, you will have to pay for the work done. The only exception to this rule is if you can prove you fired your attorney for "good cause." (See Chapter 8 for a list of "good cause" reasons.) In negotiating the terms of employment with your attorney, try to agree on payments in the event the attorney is fired. Write these terms into your agreement.

In some states your attorney can keep some of your case documents (place a "lien" on them) if the attorney is owed money by you. This is likely to create problems if you choose to pursue your case without this person, so make sure your agreement specifies that all documents pertinent to your case will be turned over to you immediately if your attorney is no longer handling the case.

RIGHTS AND RESPONSIBILITIES

The way you've selected your attorney and prepared an agreement has demonstrated to that attorney how involved you want to be in the progress of your case. If you plan to work with the attorney throughout the case, it should be no surprise that you also want the agreement to include specifics about your involvement.

Your agreement should specify your lawyer's rights and responsibilities as well as yours: who is to do what and when. The agreement should spell out how you expect to participate in the case and what you expect of your attorney. For example, this section of your agreement might specify that you expect regular updates on your case, or that you will file all documents with the courts yourself and take care of locating witnesses.

CONCLUSION

Written agreements benefit both you and the attorney by providing a concrete understanding of the terms of your relationship and the expectations on both sides. Make sure you understand this agreement before signing it. Insist on language you understand. Make it clear that you take the terms seriously because you are entrusting the attorney with your legal rights.

CHAPTER **6**

WORKING WITH YOUR LAWYER

You can't simply hand over your problem to a lawyer and sit back waiting for results—unless you don't care about the results or the cost. Regardless of the degree of involvement you choose, you have responsibilities. Certain decisions can be made by no one but you, but in addition to these minimal responsibilities you can use basic strategies to avoid misunderstandings, create a reliable record of your relationship and spot problems early.

Throughout this chapter, two pieces of advice are repeated often:

• Use your attorney's time efficiently.
• Get it in writing.

YOUR RESPONSIBILITIES

You are in a position to require that your attorney behave responsibly toward you if you fulfill the following basic client responsibilities:

• *Do what you promise.* If you have committed yourself to doing certain tasks, perform them completely and promptly. Review and pay bills when they are due.
• *Be candid.* Your lawyer can't operate effectively with half the facts. Anything important to your case will most likely

37

come out in the end. Your lawyer is better off knowing what to expect and not being "blind-sided." Also, your candor and cooperation can breed candor and cooperation on the part of the lawyer.

- *Keep your lawyer informed.* This means updating the lawyer on events that affect your case. It also means letting your lawyer know if you omitted any important information in prior consultations.

MANAGEMENT STRATEGIES

You can use any of the following strategies to keep up to date on developments and your lawyer's actions. These strategies can save you time and money as well as provide early warning of problems:

Preparation

Collect all relevant documents and organize a short written summary of facts or questions before you meet with your attorney. This can save time for both of you. It also helps make sure your questions get answered and that the discussion is focused.

Keep Notes

Make notes about what you want to discuss. This gives you a convenient way of keeping track of your talks with your attorney. Jot down the lawyer's answers on the same paper and date your notes. This creates a record to refresh your memory or to use if problems develop.

Keep Files

As soon as you have hired your attorney, set up a file for case documents. Keep a copy of your signed agreement, bills, a record of payments with the check or money order numbers noted, copies of all court papers or reports relevant to your case and your notes or letters about discussions with your attorney.

In a second file, keep your original case documents. The only times your lawyer is likely to need originals is to use them as evidence in a trial or to transfer property ownership. Except at these times, you should keep all originals and give copies to your lawyer. This file will prove useful to both you and the lawyer for ready reference, and if problems arise with your attorney you will not find yourself trying to hire another attorney at the last minute without the documents from your case file.

Write Letters of Understanding

Clients often complain about the length of time it takes to settle their case. Sometimes delay is the result of the court system, but at other times the delay is caused by the lawyer. One way to keep your lawyer's "feet to the fire" is to send letters of understanding. These restate the major points of your latest meeting or telephone conversation.

Keep the letter brief and outline the basic decisions, how tasks are to be divided and the timetable agreed upon. Make the letters sound as though you are confirming your understanding of the arrangements, not as though you distrust the lawyer. Be sure to keep a copy of these letters and your lawyer's answers, if any, as they provide you with a written record of your case history.

For example, if during your office visit your lawyer tells you of plans to search for an important expert witness and that you should collect certain documents and meet in a week to prepare questions for the witness, you might follow up such a meeting with a letter like this:

March 30, 1990

Dear Lawyer McDougall:
  I want to make sure I understood our conversation of March 29, 1990, so I'm putting it in writing. Please have your secretary call me if there is any misunderstanding on my part.
  You advised me that an orthopedic surgeon's testimony is more likely to produce a settlement than the testimony of a chiropractor would, although it will be more expensive. I am to collect all my doctor and therapy bills and be in your office next Wednesday at 1:00 P.M. You will collect the names and fee estimates of expert witnesses by then and we will draft our questions at that time.

Sincerely,
Samantha Client

Use the Telephone

Telephone consultations can be more economical than personal visits because you are more likely to get right to the point if you call. Also, you will not have to spend work time getting to your lawyer's office.

Keep in mind that your lawyer is probably billing you for telephone time and that a five-minute call may translate into a quarter of an hour of billed time. Also, your lawyer may not answer interruptive, unscheduled phone calls. To use your time best and your lawyer's time most efficiently, follow these rules:

• Call only when you have specific business.
• Ask if it is a convenient time to talk. If not, discuss how long your conversation will take and make an appointment. Ask the attorney to call you at the scheduled time.
• Keep your line clear. Be as punctual about this appointment as you would be if you were meeting in person.
• Keep a log noting when you talked and for how long. This can be compared with your itemized bill or serve as evidence should a grievance or fee dispute arise later.

• Follow up your conversation with a letter of understanding. Note when you next expect to speak or meet with the lawyer.

Ask Questions

Don't nag, but don't be afraid to ask questions, either. It's the only way to get answers and be sure you understand exactly what is happening on your case. This is critical if you are to make key decisions and to understand your lawyer's reasoning. You may find that your lawyer's answers to your questions lead you to provide information you had not thought important earlier. Questions are critical, but they should be used not as weapons but as tools for informing both of you about the problem you are working together to solve.

Get Second Opinions

When you face an important decision in your case and are unsure about why your attorney is recommending one course of action—accepting a settlement offer, for example—think about getting a second opinion.

Look for the right lawyer. It won't do you any good to find someone who is unwilling to examine a fellow lawyer's advice or who would like to take over the case. You should explain the decision or action you want advice about and make clear that you are not trying to second-guess your attorney. You want only to inform yourself about other opinions and options.

Second opinions can be valuable, but they are also expensive. They should be sought and used only when you have serious questions about what your lawyer is encouraging you to do. If you find yourself thinking about getting them more than once or twice, it may be time to consider hiring a new lawyer instead.

Consider Settling Early

If your lawyer's conduct is beginning to worry you, it may be time to consider settling your case. You need to balance the possible expenses and fees of going forward against the latest settlement offer made by the other side. If you have lost confidence in your attorney, it may be less costly for you to cut your losses.

Settling before you get what you wanted may seem like a bitter pill to swallow, but if your problems with your attorney worsen, the cost of switching lawyers or continuing to quarrel with the one you have may outweigh the amount you can get by pursuing your suit.

Of course, there are steps you can take before problems become so serious you have to consider settling early and dropping your case. The next chapter discusses these strategies.

CHAPTER 7

IF PROBLEMS
DEVELOP

If problems develop between you and your lawyer, respond to them as soon as you become aware of them. Don't ignore them and hope they will go away; if you do, they're more likely to get worse. An early talk can often solve the difficulties and save you increased worry and frustration. Remember, communicate your concerns. Neither you nor your lawyer is a mind reader.

The most common complaint clients have about their lawyers is overcharging; this is followed by neglect of the client or case. Because of the frequency of complaints in these two areas, they are discussed at length in this chapter, but remember, the techniques you use to solve these problems can be used to solve others as well.

Examples of other problems you can run into include the lawyer's failure to contact your witnesses, failure to show up for a hearing or trial, failure to prepare you for a hearing, suggesting that you perjure yourself, agreeing to a settlement without your permission, pressuring you to make a decision, stealing your money and "blackmailing" you to pay additional fees immediately before trial. All such complaints and others can often be dealt with successfully by using the strategies discussed in this chapter.

EXCESSIVE FEES

A written agreement that is clear about your lawyer's fees can prevent fee disputes from escalating. You can use the terms of your agreement as a tool to resolve difficulties. For example, if you agreed on a monthly itemized billing and no bill arrives, you can call and ask about the expected bill. This way you are both seeking to solve the problem and telegraphing your seriousness about the agreement.

OVERCHARGING

If you did take the precaution of negotiating an agreement, your first bill should not be a surprise to you. If it seems significantly higher than what you expected, you may have been charged too much for the work done. Your key to understanding whether a fee is excessive is an itemized list of what has been done, the time it took and who performed the work—a paralegal, a clerk, a secretary or your lawyer. All charges for expenses should also be itemized. If you don't have an itemized bill, write or call the lawyer and ask for one. Mention, too, that all future bills should be itemized.

OVERLAWYERING

If you are surprised by an itemized bill because of the number of hours billed, the number of procedures required, the number of phone calls made by support staff or the amount of research time spent on your case, you may be a victim of "overlawyering." Such surprises may or may not have been your lawyer's fault, but you should have been informed in advance of any developments that were likely to increase the cost of your case.

Overlawyering most commonly occurs in hourly-fee cases handled by large firms in which a senior lawyer serves as a business manager at the top of a pyramid of associate attorneys, paralegals, clerks, librarians, secretaries and other staff. These senior partners draw business to the firms and supervise the work of others. Such a system has built-in incentives for generating income through unnecessary work. Be mindful, however, that there is no guarantee small firms or solo practitioners will not overcharge or "overlawyer" as well.

WRITE A LETTER

If after careful review of your bill you conclude you have been overcharged, write a letter to your attorney questioning specific items that seem unnecessary. You should be firm but indicate a willingness to compromise. Suggest a specific dollar amount you consider fair. It is to your advantage to be reasonable and willing to negotiate.

In your letter remind the lawyer about estimates, what was said earlier about fees, or what seems fair to pay for your kind of case. Be businesslike. The best business letters recognize the value of the reader's time. They are to the point, logical, brief and objective. Stay focused on the central issues. You want your letter to be thoughtful and concise, not confrontational or disjointed. Keep a copy of the letter in your files.

If you write a letter, ask for a written response by a certain date. Two weeks is usually reasonable. Lawyers take the written word seriously. They appreciate its value as a record and its weight in any legal arena. By using it, you are meeting lawyers on their own ground, communicating the businesslike attitude you bring to the relationship and creating a record or "paper trail" should you need to take the case to fee arbitration or court later on.

TWO WHO "WON"

As an example of how this technique can work, when one client took issue with the number of hours she was billed for her case, she wrote the law firm a letter outlining her understanding of the quantity, quality and nature of the legal services she had received. She explained what she believed to be the fair value of the services, based on the firm's hourly rate of $120, then added an extra percentage to show her "good faith." She suggested cutting the original bill by 25%. The firm accepted her offer.

In another case a client was charged $34,000 for legal services on a property sale. After receiving the bill, he asked for an accounting of the hours spent on the case. It turned out the firm had spent 112 hours on his case and charged $14,000 for this time at the firm's normal rate of $125 an hour. The additional $20,000 charge had been based entirely on the value of the property sold in the transaction.

Because there was no initial agreement on fees, the law allowed the firm to collect what was "reasonable." If the client had taken his dispute to court, he would have been likely to lose. The judge would probably have ruled that a "reasonable" fee included consideration for the value of the property sold. Nevertheless, the man wrote to the lawyer, pointing out that:

- He had never agreed to pay a "reasonable fee" based on the legal definition of "reasonable."
- He had never agreed to pay an amount based on the value of the transaction.
- Much of the "value" the firm claimed to have delivered was part of the original, agreed-upon work and not an unexpected "windfall" or "bonus."
- He would accept the firm's statement of hours without question.

* He would allow the firm the highest rate that had been mentioned in their discussions—$125 an hour.

He proposed a compromise of $14,000. His lawyer wrote back:

> As I have indicated earlier, I feel that our bill was quite reasonable at $34,000. However, it is clear that there was misunderstanding with regard to the basis of our fee. It is my view that in such a situation, the blame must rest with the lawyer. Therefore, I feel that I must agree with your offer of $14,000.

If you and your lawyer do agree to a compromise, make sure a new bill is issued to reflect your agreement. Also, use this opportunity to discuss what you should do if other problems occur between you. This will show your commitment to an ongoing working relationship.

If you still cannot come to an agreement after sending letters and telephoning, you may want to take your disagreement to formal fee arbitration, or even consider firing your attorney. If so, see Chapter 8 on firing and Chapter 10 on fee disputes.

IF YOUR LAWYER NEGLECTS YOU

The second most common complaint against attorneys is neglect. Either the lawyer fails to return telephone calls, fails to meet deadlines, ignores your letters, repeatedly forgets critical facts of the case or passes you on to a clerk or paralegal each time you call or visit the office.

Some delays are beyond the control of attorneys. They are built into the court system. Nevertheless, as with unexpected fees, the reason for an unexpected delay should at least be made clear to you as soon as it is foreseen.

However, if your case is delayed because your lawyer

simply hasn't gotten around to it, you are justified in being upset. If you've been told that certain things will be done in two weeks and they are not done in three, your lawyer owes you an explanation. If a filing date is approaching and you've heard nothing from your lawyer, you have grounds to worry.

The first time such a situation occurs, telephone and tell your lawyer about your concern. Mention the timetable in your employment agreement, if you have one. Be organized and brief. Explain that you wish to discuss only your concern about the neglect, not the case itself, and that you do not expect to be billed for the time involved. Note the call in your log. Make the contact friendly and relaxed, but be firm about your concern and its seriousness.

If the problem occurs a second time, put your complaint in writing and mention your previous phone call. Keep a copy. The letter will be useful if problems persist and you want to file a grievance or malpractice case against the lawyer. Remember to ask for an answer by a specific date.

Don't accuse the lawyer in your letter, but be straightforward. Saying "I expected a bill which itemized all the charges" or asking "Is there a reason why such and such has not yet been completed?" are far less combative and far more likely to get results than more confrontational statements such as "You were supposed to send me an itemized bill" or "You are late in completing _____" Be cooperative but firm until you decide your only recourse is to fire the attorney.

MULTIPLE PROBLEMS

If several serious problems have developed over time, schedule an appointment. Tell the lawyer in advance that you want to discuss how the relationship is working, that you don't want to be charged for the time, and that you want to meet on neutral ground—not in the lawyer's office and not in your office or house.

At this meeting, encourage a candid exchange about your expectations that are not being met. You may both feel comfortable modifying your agreement, writing one if you didn't already do so or ending the employment. However, be careful about letting the lawyer go if doing so will jeopardize your case or leave you facing a long delay.

THE EXPECTATIONS GAME

When judging your lawyer's work against your expectations, make sure you aren't falling prey to the following common misperceptions:

"Your lawyer should be your friend." Clients often have to reveal intimate facts, feelings or thoughts to their lawyers, information normally revealed only to close relations and friends. Don't make the mistake of thinking such confidences turn your lawyer into your best friend. Remember, this is a business relationship. If your lawyer becomes your friend outside your employment relationship, fine. But don't expect or rely on this "friendship" in dealing with your legal concern. You're paying your lawyer for legal expertise, not sympathy.

"You're being sold out." Some clients believe that because their lawyer is urging them to settle out of court, the lawyer has been bought by the enemy. Settlement does not mean you've "lost." Most cases are settled before trial. You hired your lawyer to assess the strengths and weaknesses of your case and give advice about alternatives. If your lawyer urges you to settle, it may be because the cost of pursuing the case outweighs the probable benefits.

If your attorney recommends settlement, ask for a comparison of the costs and likely benefits of pursuing the case further. It's best to get this in writing, too. Don't ever accept a settlement offer unless you understand it fully and have read the settlement agreement carefully. If you have doubts, don't sign until they are cleared up.

"If you lose, it's your lawyer's fault." This may be the case, but don't assume it is. Paying for legal representation doesn't guarantee you will win. Sometimes a case is weak and the odds are against your winning. If so, mediation may get you a better settlement than a lawsuit. Sometimes the law or its interpretation changes and what your lawyer believed was a strong case is abruptly weakened by court action a few days before your trial. Sometimes judges make mistakes or misapply the law despite a lawyer's best efforts.

In fact, the system of courtroom litigation almost guarantees the opposite of victory: that someone will lose. Clients usually think their case is watertight, that they are in the right and deserve to win. They believe the courts exist to give them all they are due. The difficulty is that this is true for both sides of every argument, and it is impossible for both sides to get everything they want. As a result, taking a case into court involves risk: in effect, you are asking someone else to decide what is right for you, instead of forging a solution yourself through compromise or negotiation.

"It'll be over in a month." Lawyers aren't magicians. They are caught in the same crowded court backlogs and built-in procedural delays as you are. In most cases hiring a lawyer won't speed up the process. In some situations, such as writing a will, drafting a lease or settling a real estate sale, a month may be reasonable, but few other legal matters allow for such speedy resolution whether you hire a lawyer or not. Your case will never be over in a month if it involves litigation or a hearing, and some civil cases do not reach trial until five years after the complaint was filed.

NEGOTIATE YOUR DIFFERENCES

If strategies for managing your attorney-client relationship fail and you are still faced with problems, try resolving them through negotiation. The most successful negotiators are well organized, present themselves convincingly and have prepared a compromise position. Unless you are ready to fire your attorney, appear cooperative. After all, you are still hoping the lawyer will continue to work on your case and produce the results you want.

Everyone uses negotiating skills every day. It's how you get what you want from others without resorting to force, a process of communication in a mutual search for agreement when two sides have shared interests but different positions. Your goal with your lawyer is to maintain your relationship while fashioning a solution to the problem that is agreeable to both of you. Here are some tips for successful negotiation:

- Sort out what the problem is and try to generate several possible solutions before meeting with the lawyer. Write down the facts that support your understanding of the problem and your possible solutions so you'll remember this information when you meet. This will give you room to find a solution on which both of you can agree.

- Set aside a time to meet when neither of you are rushed. You will be able to concentrate better than if you try to resolve the issue by telephone or when either of you is busy with other projects.

- Don't confuse personalities with issues. If you concentrate on your underlying interests instead of blame, you're more likely to come to a resolution. Think of yourselves as problem solvers concentrating on the future, not the past. This does not mean you have to avoid emotion. Describe how you feel, but don't act out anger or frustration in a way that minimizes your chances of resolving the dispute.

- Discuss your perceptions with the lawyer. You may find that sorting out what was promised from what actually happened will help you arrive at an understanding.
- Use objective standards to decide what is fair. If, for example, what you want most is that your divorce be final by a certain date, bring to the bargaining table whatever information you can to demonstrate that your suggested resolution is reasonable.
- Listen carefully and acknowledge that you have heard the lawyer's position. Listening is a negotiator's most valuable tool.
- Write down the solution so you both know you agree on its terms. Also, a written record of it will help avoid future misunderstandings.

DON'T THREATEN TO SUE

You may decide you want to sue your lawyer for malpractice or file a grievance. Regardless of this decision, threatening such actions is not an effective way of getting a lawyer to "shape up." Instead, threats are likely to cause an irreparable rift. Besides, it can take three years or more for the suit or grievance complaint to be settled, and your lawyer knows it. Time will not be on your side.

If you have reached such an impasse, it is time to consider firing your lawyer or dropping your case. Instead of threatening to sue, put your reasons for preparing to fire your lawyer in writing and state that you will fire the lawyer unless the problem is solved. Specify the actions you want your attorney to take in order not to be fired. But remember, only when your efforts at negotiating have failed is it time to consider the more drastic step of firing your lawyer.

CHAPTER 8

PARTING WITH YOUR LAWYER

A client can fire an attorney, but an attorney can't fire a client. That is how it is supposed to work. The lawyer can, however, withdraw under certain conditions. Indeed, a lawyer is required to withdraw from a case if he or she cannot represent a client competently.

Each state has different laws about this, but common reasons for requiring lawyers to withdraw include poor health, prior commitments to other cases that interfere with their ability to give attention to yours, conflict of interest and personal problems, such as alcoholism or marital stress. An attorney can also withdraw from your case if you don't pay your bill or if you refuse to cooperate, for example by not showing up for a meeting or by concealing facts essential to the case.

Despite the consumer protection implied in these laws, their practical effect is that lawyers can withdraw almost anytime they choose. If no lawsuit has been filed, your lawyer can withdraw simply by telling you so. After a lawsuit has been filed, the lawyer must ask the court's permission before withdrawing, but such motions to withdraw are almost always approved by the court. They are denied only in extreme circumstances, such as when trial is scheduled the next day and your lawyer has already been granted several postponements.

If your lawyer asks you to agree to a withdrawal, weigh whether you want to file a lawsuit or formal complaint. If you do, it is better not to consent to the withdrawal, even though the chances are that the court will allow the lawyer to drop your case anyway.

Whether or not you agree, ask the lawyer to send you a written notice of intent to withdraw and to state the reasons. (It's best if you included a requirement for this in your original employment agreement.) If your lawyer refuses to give you written notice, make a note of the time and date of the oral notice and include notes on the reasons given. This way you will have a record should you later decide to file a grievance with the state lawyer disciplinary agency or to sue your lawyer.

When lawyers are allowed to withdraw, most states require them to help you find a new lawyer, to cooperate with your new attorney, to refund costs or fees that have not been earned and to return your case file. Despite these requirements, however, lawyers rarely volunteer to do any of these things. If you want them done, you'll probably have to assert your rights.

FIRING YOUR LAWYER

Your freedom to fire your lawyer is almost absolute. You are not required to have a good reason. The only time you are not allowed to fire your lawyer is when you attempt to use the firing to delay a court proceeding or otherwise to manipulate a delay for your benefit.

The fact that you are free to fire your lawyer doesn't mean you should use that freedom at the first sign of minor disagreement. You should carefully consider what firing your lawyer can cost you. The further along your case is, the more serious a step firing becomes. It will cost time and money and can seriously jeopardize your case. It should be considered only after you've tried diligently to remedy your problems with the lawyer or in cases of serious misconduct.

There are three major reasons not to fire a lawyer:

- Hiring and educating a new lawyer about your case is usually time-consuming and expensive.
- You may not find another lawyer willing to take the case.
- Delay may irreparably damage your case, for example by forcing you to miss critical deadlines.

Before firing your lawyer, talk over your concerns to make sure you understand the lawyer's side. If you are not sure whether you should fire the lawyer, consider getting a second opinion. Ask a staff person at the local bar grievance committee (see Appendix IV). You may even want to ask another lawyer. It costs money to hire another lawyer to review your original lawyer's conduct, but you do need to make an informed decision.

It's a good idea to try to shop for a new lawyer before firing your old one so that you won't have to drop the case or represent yourself. Any lawyer you interview will ask if you already have representation. Tell the truth: that you are dissatisfied with your present attorney and why. This may make some attorneys wary of taking your case or unwilling to talk with you until your lawyer is fired, but your honesty can prevent the same kind of problems arising with your next attorney.

FIRING FOR "GOOD CAUSE"

Although you can fire your lawyer for almost any reason, state laws also set out "good cause" reasons for firing. If you have such reasons, you may not have to pay fees. Most "good cause" reasons are also grounds for discipline or a malpractice suit against your lawyer. The laws differ from state to state, but most of them include the following "good cause" reasons:

- *Aggravated neglect.* For example, your lawyer repeatedly misses deadlines and hearing dates and refuses to answer letters or return telephone calls.
- *Breach of confidentiality.* For example, after you have discussed with your lawyer your suspicions about your spouse's infidelity, you discover the lawyer has talked about those suspicions with fellow country club members.
- *Illegal action.* For example, your lawyer tells you to lie about your case under oath or suggests that you bribe a witness.
- *Failure to supervise staff.* For example, a casual acquaintance of yours is told about your divorce by your lawyer's secretary or a law clerk fails to file court papers on time.
- *Incompetence.* Your lawyer's actions reveal a pattern of repeated errors, such as failure to file court papers on time, having to refile papers that were incorrectly completed or filed, failure to learn current law related to your case, repeatedly trying to use inadmissible evidence, failure to call witnesses, being unprepared at hearings or settlement conferences, or missing the deadline for filing suit.
- *Morally offensive behavior.* Some examples: your lawyer sexually harasses you; swears at you, the judge, your opponent or the other lawyer; or arrives drunk at hearings, settlement conferences or appointments. Simple rudeness is not considered "good cause" for firing a lawyer, however.
- *Conflicts of interest.* For example, your lawyer agrees to a settlement you did not approve or has a personal financial interest that conflicts with your case. Having lunch with

your opponent's attorney, however does not constitute a conflict of interest.

• *Breach of fiduciary duty.* When you entrust money or property, including your legal rights, to your lawyer, the lawyer is said to have a "fiduciary" duty to you. That duty is breached if, for example, your lawyer invests your daughter's trust fund in an extremely risky venture or fails to remind you to rewrite your will after major changes in your state's inheritance tax laws. Given the trust you have placed in your attorney, any significant failure to exercise good judgment qualifies as a breach of fiduciary duty.

• *Code of ethics violations.* Each state has what is called a "code of professional responsibility" or "model rules of professional conduct" that govern lawyers' behavior. Examples of typical violations: your lawyer puts your trust funds in a private bank account; is convicted of a felony; lies on a license application; or uses knowledge about your case to represent your opponent later on.

If you have considered the pros and cons and have decided to discharge your lawyer, write a letter stating your reasons and schedule a meeting to discuss them. Make arrangements for paying the final bill if you agree that you owe the lawyer money. If you disagree with the lawyer over how much you owe and the lawyer threatens to keep your file if you don't pay, remember that paying now may get your files back but will probably make it more difficult to negotiate a fee reduction or to get the lawyer to agree to fee arbitration later on. The best thing is to have preserved all your options in fee disputes by keeping your own file of all original documents from the beginning.

CHAPTER 9

CLIENT SECURITY TRUST FUNDS

People who have been the victims of attorney misconduct frequently ask what they can do about it. All too often the answer is, not much. There are four recourses:

- If the lawyer stole the client's money, the client can seek reimbursement from the state's client security trust fund.
- If the client wants the lawyer disciplined for misconduct, a grievance complaint can be filed with the state or local bar association.
- If the lawyer's fee is disputed, the client can ask for fee arbitration.
- The client can sue the lawyer for malpractice.

You do not have to fire your attorney in order to have access to any of these recourses. You may use them even after the lawyer has successfully provided the services you bought. Your degree of satisfaction with the outcome may influence whether or not you seek formal remedies for complaints you have about your attorney, but you should never let that final outcome be the only determining factor. While the four options may seem, at first glance, to provide considerable remedies, several factors keep them from being of major benefit to most consumers.

First, lawyers are self-regulating. Lawyers, often under state and local bar associations, run the attorney grievance committees, client security trust funds and fee arbitration committees. Thus each option for consumer redress involves submitting your complaint primarily to other attorneys. In most cases the process takes place in secret and your right to appeal is limited. Of late these and other programs to protect consumers have come under increasing public scrutiny and pressure for reform.

This is not to say that the procedures already in place aren't worth pursuing. If you believe you have been the victim of attorney misconduct, you should fully explore all your options. Remember, using one recourse doesn't prevent you from using one or more of the others. In fact, in some instances you may want to arbitrate a lower fee, seek reimbursement of stolen money from the client security trust fund, file a grievance complaint with the bar *and* file a malpractice suit. This chapter explains client security trust funds and the next three chapters discuss the other alternatives.

CLIENT SECURITY TRUST FUNDS

One of the clearest cases of attorney misconduct is stealing a client's money. Because such theft is obviously flagrant misconduct and erodes public confidence in attorneys, many state bar associations have established client security trust funds. Money for these funds is collected from attorneys in the state, typically as part of their bar dues, and used to reimburse clients.

Lawyers can steal from clients in a number of ways. Most often an attorney responsible for the money in a trust fund or an estate keeps it—or "comingles" it—with personal money. In one dramatic case, a New York attorney stole more than $1.5 million from more than a hundred clients in this way before being discovered.

In other thefts an attorney may accept a retainer fee but never do any work on a case and refuse to refund the money. Or an attorney may simply pocket the money won in a lawsuit. This is easily done because attorneys generally have settlement checks made payable to them so they can deduct their fees before forwarding the remainder to you.

To be reimbursed for money stolen or misappropriated by your lawyer, simply apply to your state bar's client security trust fund. Appendix IV lists fund addresses and phone numbers. However, recognize that all programs limit the amount refundable. The maximum that will be refunded on a single case varies from state to state. If your loss exceeds the limit, your only recourse to get the rest back is to sue the lawyer. This may be impossible or pointless, however, because by the time you become aware of the theft, your lawyer is likely to have fled the state or gone bankrupt.

FILING A TRUST CLAIM

To file a claim, contact your state's trust fund committee and ask for the rules for filing. Usually you cannot hire a lawyer to help you file your claim because lawyers are not allowed to accept payment for helping present a claim. You will be asked to fill out a form. You should attach copies of any letters, bills, or receipts and a brief summary of the complaint. Keep a copy of your form and the originals of any attachments you submit.

The fund committee is composed only of lawyers. They review your claim and contact the lawyer in question. They may also ask you to supply further information. No hearing is held, and the claim and evidence are not made public. If your claim is found to have merit, the committee will order reimbursement, but it reserves the right to reimburse only part of the money stolen. In many states, you can't appeal the committee's decision. If the committee turns you down or only partially reimburses you, your only recourse is to file a lawsuit against your lawyer.

If your claim is rejected, you will receive a letter advising you of the rejection, but depending on your state's rules, you may not have the right to have the reasons for the committee's decision stated in writing. In some states, if you have also filed a disciplinary complaint against your lawyer, the claim to the security fund will be delayed until the disciplinary complaint is settled. Also, information from the disciplinary committee can affect the outcome of your fund claim.

During its first ten years, California's fund paid out up to 67% of claims each year, and typical claims ranged between $2,500 and $5,000. The state bar associations' unreviewable authority to administer these funds is coming under increasing challenge, but until payments from the fund are viewed as a right and not as distributed by the "grace" of the bar, to quote many state fund's rules, these challenges are unlikely to succeed. You have nothing to lose by seeking compensation from the fund, but be aware of the limitations.

CHAPTER **10**

FEE DISPUTES

Among the most common complaints filed with state bar associations is that lawyer fees are too high for the work done. In response, most state and some local bars have created out-of-court arbitration forums for resolving lawyer-client fee disputes. These special arbitration programs have names like D.C. Attorney-Client Arbitration Board, New Jersey Fee Arbitration System, and Illinois Committee on Voluntary Fee Arbitration.

The advantages of taking a disputed fee to arbitration is that it is quick, it is considerably less expensive than taking the dispute to court, and almost half the states with fee arbitration programs require that at least some nonlawyers serve on hearing panels. Of equal importance, if your lawyer takes you to court to collect a fee and wins, you could end up paying the costs, including your lawyer's own attorney fees.

Fee arbitration offers clients and their lawyers the opportunity to resolve fee disputes in front of a panel of arbitrators. The bar-selected panel listens to testimony, examines evidence and decides whether to uphold or reduce the lawyer's requested fee. Some decisions are binding, while others are only advisory. If binding, they can be enforced by a court. When both sides agree, most fee disputes can be arbitrated. The only exceptions are fees set or approved by a court, fees already the subject of a lawsuit filed by either the client or the lawyer, and fees based on malpractice or misconduct.

A 1987 HALT survey found that the bars of thirty states and the District of Columbia offer fee arbitration statewide. In fourteen other states, the bars offer arbitration only at the local level, and in six states (Alabama, Arkansas, Louisiana, Nebraska, South Dakota and West Virginia) they do not offer it at all. Appendix IV lists fee arbitration programs.

VOLUNTARY VERSUS MANDATORY ARBITRATION

Participating bar associations offer two types of arbitration: voluntary and mandatory. Voluntary, the more common, requires that you and your lawyer agree to participate in binding arbitration. Either side is free to refuse. In mandatory arbitration, the lawyer is required to submit to binding arbitration if you request it. (California has a hybrid of the two systems: the lawyer has to participate, but both the client and lawyer can choose whether the arbitrators' decision will be advisory or binding.)

ARBITRATORS

If the bar accepts your application, it will give you the name or names of the arbitrators assigned to hear your case. A panel of one to three arbitrators will be chosen, the number depending on your state's rules, the size of the fee in dispute and occasionally your own preference.

Arbitrators are appointed by a bar administrator. If you are worried that your arbitrators may not be impartial, do some research when you get their names. In particular, try to determine whether they are members of the same bar association or law firm as the lawyer whose bill you're contesting. If you have reason to suspect that one or more arbitrators' judgment will be biased, you can challenge their appointment.

THE HEARING

When membership of the arbitration panel is settled, you and your lawyer will be notified of a hearing date. If you wish, you can be represented at the hearing by a lawyer, although most people choose to represent themselves. The chair of the arbitration panel will explain the process, then give you a chance to tell your side of the story.

You can present witnesses and any documentary evidence you have. The lawyer with whom you are in dispute is then allowed to do the same. Each of you can cross-examine the other. The rules of procedure are often quite informal, and arbitrators may ask questions at any time. If more than one hearing is needed, the chair will probably try to arrange the next meeting before you leave the room. When the arbitrators have no more questions and no more meetings are needed, they will officially close the hearing.

You will be notified in writing of the arbitrators' decision. If that decision is binding and goes against you, the lawyer has the legal right to force you to pay. Similarly, you have the right to a refund if you have already paid a fee that is ruled unreasonable.

A binding decision cannot be appealed in court unless a procedural error was made during arbitration. This means that you cannot appeal simply because you don't agree with the decision; however, you *can* appeal if you can prove that the arbitrators committed fraud, exceeded their authority, were biased or failed to follow the procedural rules.

If things go smoothly, the whole process should take sixty to ninety days. Usually you are not charged anything for the services, but a few state bars charge a filing fee of $15 to $25, which may be waived if you are unable to pay. Some local arbitration programs may charge more or demand a percentage of the fee in dispute, but the process should still cost considerably less than litigation.

IF YOUR LAWYER REFUSES

In some places where arbitration is voluntary, if your lawyer refuses to arbitrate, the bar will help you pursue your case. It may give you free advice or an advisory opinion from the arbitration panel, or even appoint a free lawyer to help you file a lawsuit over the disputed fee.

About half of the state bars with voluntary arbitration centers, however, do not help in any way if your lawyer refuses to arbitrate. In those states, if your lawyer refuses to arbitrate and you want a refund, your only option is to litigate. You can also file a complaint with the state agency handling discipline, but, as is discussed in Chapter 11, these agencies rarely provide refunds and handle only allegations of extreme overcharging. You might also decide to write a letter to the editor of your local newspaper.

QUESTIONS TO ASK

If you have a dispute over your lawyer's bill and want to try arbitration, call your area bar association office to determine:

• Are arbitration hearings formal? If the procedure is too formal, you may not want to handle it on your own. On the other hand, formality can mean the panel is serious about its operation and that cronyism is kept to a minimum.

- Is there a formal administrative structure with someone in charge of the operation? Make sure that what goes under the banner of "arbitration" is not simply "mediation" in another lawyer's office—a signal that cronyism may be at play.
- Are there incentives to encourage lawyers to agree to arbitrate?
- Do laypeople serve as arbitrators?
- How much is the filing fee? Is this fee refundable? Under what circumstances?
- Is the arbitration binding?
- Does the bar publish a brochure describing the rules and procedures in your state?
- What should a request for arbitration include?
- How many arbitrators are clients allowed to challenge? Is there a deadline for challenging them?

CHAPTER 11

ATTORNEY DISCIPLINE

Every state has a disciplinary or grievance committee charged with making sure that only honest, competent lawyers are licensed. Over half of these agencies are run by state bar associations. In the remaining states, such agencies are independent, although state bar associations typically have considerable influence over who sits on the governing board, who is hired as the head of the agency and how complaints are processed.

The rules by which these agencies operate are spelled out in the state's code of professional responsibility or rules of professional conduct. This document is usually based on a model written by the American Bar Association. Either the highest court of the state enforces the rules directly, or else it supervises state agency enforcement and provides judicial oversight and interpretation of ethical standards.

You can get a copy of the code of professional responsibility for your state from a public law library or the state bar association. In general, most agencies can discipline attorneys found guilty of:

- Acts of moral turpitude—felonies or misdemeanors involving malice or lying
- Dishonesty, fraud or misrepresentation
- Mixing a client's money with the attorney's own funds ("comingling") or stealing from a client

- Accepting employment when the work may be affected by a personal, financial or business interest
- Repeated failure to act competently

If you complain about a lawyer to your state or local disciplinary committee, the lawyer can be disciplined, but only rarely can you receive compensation through this procedure, even if your complaint is determined to be valid. In fact, less than 5% of all complaints result in disciplinary action.

There are four basic types of discipline (although not every state uses all four):

Private Reprimand.   Only you, the panel and the disciplined lawyer are told what happened. In effect the lawyer is confidentially told to "go and sin no more." This occurs in about 2.5% of all cases.

Public Reprimand.   A "public" notice of the reprimand is published, usually in the state bar journal or newspaper distributed to lawyers licensed in the state. The lawyer may be embarrassed among colleagues, but the information will reach only the limited readership of the journal. About 1.5% of all cases result in a public reprimand.

Suspension.   A suspension can range from a few days to several years. During this time, the lawyer is not licensed to practice law in that state. This occurs in less than 1% of all cases.

Disbarment.   This is the severest penalty available. It is used only when an attorney is found guilty of repeated or gross misconduct or is convicted of a felony. An attorney who is disbarred may not practice law in that state, though another state may allow the attorney to practice. In most states, a disbarred attorney may apply for reinstatement five years after being disbarred. Less than one fifth of 1% of all cases result in disbarment.

You should consider the following factors before filing a complaint:

- In about half the states the reviewing panels arc composed entirely of lawyers.
- In every state but Oregon clients have no right to know how many complaints have been filed against a lawyer.
- In most states the proceedings are secret, and even the decisions are kept secret unless they result in a public reprimand, suspension or disbarment.
- If no public action is taken, in most states the complaining client is sworn to secrecy.
- Usually the attorney can appeal the decision, but the client cannot.
- The committees' powers are limited to the punishments at their disposal.
- Investigative resources are limited and long delays are common. It can take years to handle a case. In California, for example, four-year delays are routine.
- An attorney may be guilty of malpractice and still not violate the state's ethical rules. Rules are very narrowly drawn because they are intended to uphold only minimum licensing standards.

Many people considering a grievance complaint against their lawyer are worried that the lawyer will sue them for defamation. Such retaliation suits have been made illegal in some states, and where they are not illegal the court will often recognize their intent and take it into consideration. The main reason for filing such a suit is to discourage you from pursuing your complaint. If this happens to you, contact your state disciplinary committee and ask what your rights are.

WHY COMPLAIN?

Because filing a grievance seldom results in discipline and rarely brings the client any monetary relief, you might ask why anyone should bother filing a complaint. One answer is that if injured clients didn't complain, statistics like those already cited in this chapter would not be available for use in demanding adequate consumer protection.

An example: in 1985 a four-year scandal in Connecticut culminated in sweeping legislative reforms. A local disciplinary committee had failed to act adequately against the attorneys for their mishandling of a $38 million estate even though the three attorneys and a judge had already been publicly criticized by another judge, a judicial ethics panel, and a legislative committee for stealing an elderly woman's property, invading her privacy and charging more than $500,000 in fees while wrestling for four years over control of her estate.

Even after media coverage of the case and the judge's resignation under threat of impeachment, the grievance committee delayed action for fifteen months. It was only after a court ordered the committee to act that it recommended a private reprimand for one of the lawyers and public reprimands for the other two. When a state legislator tried to protest the leniency, he was given a ten-day jail sentence for contempt of court. Public and legislative outrage over the jailing led to a major reform of Connecticut's grievance process, including nonlawyer involvement and public hearings.

Complaining about your attorney's misconduct can also help assure that future clients of the same lawyer are spared your experience. Your case may be the fifth time your attorney's name has come up in such proceedings, establishing a pattern the committee can't ignore. Also, pursuing your complaint can bolster a claim that you fired your attorney for good cause and therefore shouldn't be required to pay fees. Finally, your complaint could contribute to making the committee more accountable to consumers.

HOW TO FILE A COMPLAINT

Filing a complaint is easy—especially if you have been diligent about keeping good records—and it costs you nothing. You may hire an attorney to represent you, but most people don't because it is rare to get money even if you "win." Follow these steps:
- Contact your state or local attorney grievance or disciplinary committee (see Appendix IV) and ask for a complaint form if they have one, a copy of their brochure on the process and a copy of the rules.
- Fill out the forms or prepare a brief written summary of your complaint. If the complaint form does not give you adequate space to explain your side, attach additional sheets.
- Enclose *copies* (not originals) of bills, letters, receipts, case documents and any other documentation that supports your claim.
- Keep a copy of your complaint and the originals of any attachments or enclosures.

Complaints are screened by agency staff to determine whether they allege misconduct under the state's code. Complaints that are not dismissed after the initial screening are investigated. The investigation always includes asking the lawyer named in the complaint for a response to your claims. The agency will allow at least two weeks for that response. The investigation can include gathering documents and conducting interviews. However, the agency often makes its decision based solely on the information you and your lawyer have provided, so it is important to present your case well when you file a complaint. It may well be your last chance to offer information.

Alternatively, you may be asked for further information or notified of a hearing time and place. Approximately 10% of all complaints reach a hearing stage. If you do have a hearing, your complaint will usually be heard by three panelists, most often three lawyers or two lawyers and one nonlawyer. Panelists are selected by the agency from a pool of volunteers.

Your role in the hearing is that of a witness in the agency's "case" against the lawyer. However, you should still prepare for the hearing by:

- Organizing your evidence and arguments
- Gathering copies of all relevant documents
- Preparing a clear presentation, using your written records to cite specific instances of misconduct

Rules for hearings vary significantly from state to state. In general, the rules of evidence don't apply. Most states do not allow you to ask the lawyer questions, but do allow the lawyer to question you. Some states don't even allow you to be present during the lawyer's presentation or to call on witnesses. Either person can be represented by a lawyer, but need not be.

After the hearing, the panel will deliberate. The panel can either dismiss the complaint, give a private reprimand or recommend that the lawyer be publicly disciplined. A recommendation of public discipline will usually be reviewed by the agency's governing board. Some governing boards also review private reprimands. Few dismissals of complaints are reviewed. If the governing board approves a recommendation for public discipline, a formal charge is filed with the court.

The court assigns a referee to process the charge. In some states the referee may hold another hearing, but it usually does not include calling witnesses and presenting evidence. Instead, both sides present oral arguments—the disciplinary agency argues in support of the recommendation and the lawyer is allowed to present a defense.

The referee can decide to approve, reject or modify the agency's recommendation. Usually, however, the recommendation is approved without question. You will be sent a letter notifying you if discipline is to be imposed. In some states you are sent a written decision that includes the panel's reasoning. This information is made public only if public discipline has been approved.

In some states you are not allowed to appeal a decision but the lawyer can appeal. You are not allowed to offer evidence at this appeal hearing, but you may be able to attend, as appeals are usually public.

CHAPTER 12

SUING YOUR LAWYER

If your lawyer is guilty of misconduct, chances are you'd like to get your money back for the damage the lawyer caused. If you sue your lawyer for malpractice and win, you can be awarded money and sometimes attorney fees. However, deciding whether to sue for legal malpractice is rarely that simple.

You should consider six factors before deciding. They include:

Time.   Legal malpractice cases can be complex. Depending on the complexity, it could take years to settle or to pursue in court. Malpractice lawyers say cases take an average of two years, with some taking up to six.

Cost.   Pursuing a malpractice case costs money. You'll pay lawyer fees if you win and expenses whether you win or lose. Fees and expenses can run extremely high, depending on the facts of your case, your negotiations when hiring your malpractice lawyer, and how the lawyer you are suing (or the malpractice insurance carrier) decides to fight the case. Make sure you know the financial, emotional and other costs of suing and balance them against a realistic assessment of what you can expect to win. Unfortunately, it's rarely cost effective to take a legal malpractice case to court unless you have a good chance of winning at least $10,000. Some lawyers even say they won't take cases unless they have a good chance of winning $50,000.

Energy. If you have already been burned by one lawyer, you may find it difficult to work with another. Assess your ability to take another crack at the legal system, given your past experiences. If you decide to pursue your case primarily because you're angry or want revenge, chances are that alone won't sustain you through the years these cases can take. Consider filing a grievance complaint instead, or writing a letter to the editor of your local newspaper.

Chances of Success. Assess your chances of success carefully. Remember, the legal system is primarily set up only to compensate you with money for your losses or injury. Weigh all the financial details. Consider getting a second legal opinion, both on your chances of winning and on the amount you're likely to win. Although cases are never certain, lawyering is a business, and lawyers should be able to estimate this for you: it's what they do before they decide whether to take a case.

In 1986 the American Bar Association's National Legal Malpractice Data Center analyzed about 30,000 legal malpractice claims filed with insurance carriers from 1983 to 1985. It reported that:

- Clients received no compensation in 63.3% of the claims.
- Fewer than 30% of the claims led to lawsuits.
- Clients who don't settle out of court win in court only 1.2% of the time.
- Extremely few clients ever receive compensation over $1,000.

Difficulty Finding a Lawyer. Members of the legal profession traditionally have been unwilling to sue their fellow lawyers, and those willing to do so are picky about the cases they take because malpractice cases are hard to win. However, insurance actuaries report that claims against lawyers are increasing 20% a year. And as the number of claims rise, so does the number of lawyers who handle such cases.

It may take time to round up prospects. In some areas of the country you may find it all but impossible to get a lawyer to take your case.[1] When you generate your list of lawyers, be sure to choose some who practice in a different town or county than the lawyer you want to sue. Most lawyers will not sue another lawyer who is probably a member of the same local bar association or whom they see frequently in court.

Other Options. Consider alternatives to suing. Using one of these options may resolve your dispute with less time, money and stress, and in most cases will not prevent you from suing later should you choose to. Standard alternatives to litigation include direct negotiation, mediation, arbitration and small claims court. You can also complain to your state's disciplinary agency, file a claim with a client security fund or arbitrate a fee dispute.

Small claims court may be an alternative if your claim is for an appropriate amount. These courts were set up to allow people to bring smaller legal claims to an efficient, inexpensive, informal setting hospitable to consumers. You do not need a lawyer to take a case to small claims court, although most states don't forbid it. The major limitations are that you can only sue for maximum amounts up to $1000 to $5,000, depending on the rules in your state.[2]

---

[1] *Directory of Lawyers Who Sue Lawyers,* Kay Ostberg and George Milko in association with HALT, 1989. Available from HALT.

[2] If you decide to try this option, refer to *Small Claims Court,* Theresa Meehan Rudy in association with HALT, Random House, 1990. It provides a step-by-step guide to bringing a case in small claims courts. It also identifies the limit on the amount you can sue for in each state.

PROVING YOUR CASE

Malpractice law is in flux. Although U.S. courts have recognized the right to sue for malpractice since 1796, this right flows from common law, which is derived from previous court decisions, not from the laws written by legislatures or in constitutions. The recent increase in malpractice cases means that courts are constantly reformulating this body of law. The good news is that the trend is to expand clients' rights to compensation.

Because the right to sue for malpractice derives from common law, each court is guided by previous "opinions" or "holdings" of the state's courts. That means the law varies from state to state. The facts of your case must be weighed in light of your state courts' interpretations of the law.

The most common grounds for which clients sue lawyers are that their case was handled negligently or that the terms of your client attorney agreement were broken (breach of contract). Negligence and breach of contract suits are called "malpractice" cases and differ from suits based on theories of intentional misconduct—such as theft, fraud or misrepresentation—which are discussed at the end of the chapter.

From the client's perspective, the primary difference between suing for negligence and suing for breach of contract is that the deadline for filing with the court may be different. (See "Defenses" below.)

Regardless what tack you take, winning a case is far from easy. To prove either negligence or breach of contract, every state requires that you show:
- You had a client-attorney relationship.
- The lawyer acted in a way that violated a duty to you.
- The lawyer's violation of that duty caused you injury.
- You suffered monetary loss because of your injuries.

The Client-Attorney Relationship

In most instances you must give evidence that the lawyer was representing you personally in a legal matter when it was mishandled. However, a growing number of states also allow some "nonclients" to sue. Perhaps the most common example would be a beneficiary of a will who sues the lawyer who mishandled the drafting of the will. Although the beneficiary never hired the lawyer, a direct financial loss resulted from the malpractice.

It is usually easy to prove that a lawyer was representing you, especially if you have copies of bills you paid. Courts have even found the necessary relationship when no fee was charged. To establish that a relationship existed, you can:

- Get the lawyer to acknowledge handling your case.
- Produce a copy of your agreement or a bill.
- Testify or otherwise provide evidence that the lawyer gave you legal advice that amounted to more than casual social conversation. (For example, you could give evidence of work such as paperwork that was done for you.)
- Show you had a good reason to rely on the lawyer's promise to handle your legal matter.
- Show that the lawyer took legal actions in your name.

Breach of Duty

Courts have held that you have a right to expect your lawyer to use "ordinary" skill, knowledge and diligence— ordinary, that is, compared to other lawyers'. This is called a "reasonable lawyer" standard.

If you have signed an employment agreement with the lawyer you are suing, it can expand or limit this duty. For example, your agreement may include a clause that requires that the task be completed within two months. If the matter is not completed in two months, this would be a breach. For the most part, however, even when you have a written agreement, it usually incorporates a "reasonable lawyer" standard.

You almost always need at least one expert witness to testify that your lawyer did not live up to the "reasonable lawyer" standard. Your expert is the key to supporting your claim that the lawyer's conduct was more serious than an "honest mistake" or "mere error in judgment."

The only instance when you would not need an expert is when the misconduct is obvious. For example, a judge is likely to find that, no matter how many lawyers make a general practice of missing court filing deadlines, this conduct falls below minimum acceptable standards and is a breach of duty.

Each state uses one or more of four versions of the "reasonable lawyer" standard. Depending on the state, your lawyer's performance may be compared to that of other lawyers in the locality, in the same state, nationwide or nationwide among lawyers who specialize in a particular area of law. As to the last, states are only now beginning to recognize that lawyers often specialize and that their clients have a right to expect that specialists will be held to a higher, "expert" standard.

Your attorney's duty also includes an obligation to follow your instructions "faithfully." This requires, for example, that your attorney accept or turn down a settlement offer according to your wishes, even when the attorney believes your decision is not in your own best interest. It also includes every major decision made as the case progresses. The only exception to this duty is that your attorney is not bound to follow your instructions on tactical and strategic decisions related to actual litigation.

There is a clear breach of duty if:
• Many appointments, hearings or court dates were missed.
• The client-attorney agreement was violated.

- Appropriate research wasn't done.
- The filing deadline (statute of limitations) was missed.

There is not necessarily a breach of duty if:
- The lawyer made an "honest mistake" or "error in judgment."
- You lost the case.
- The lawyer did not file an appeal.
- The lawyer was disciplined for ethical violations.

For specific information about what is considered a breach of duty in specific areas of law, such as family or property law, refer to Mallen and Smith's volumes, *Legal Malpractice* (see Appendix VI) or consult with a lawyer.

Proving Fault

You must establish that you suffered an injury that was caused, at least in part, by your lawyer's breach of duty. Most states hold that you don't have to prove that the lawyer was the *only* cause of your loss, but the lawyer must be shown directly responsible for it. Lawyers would say you must prove that but for the lawyer's breach, a loss would not have occurred. In plain English, that translates to—prove it was the lawyer's fault.

Establishing "causation" can be either simple or almost impossible, depending on the misconduct involved. Be warned: lawyers who defend against malpractice claims will almost always argue that the misconduct was not directly related to the injury—that is, that they were not at fault.

To establish what lawyers call proximate causation, you must show that your lawyer's misconduct directly caused your loss. This can be quite difficult, as the following example shows.

You are sued for a slip-and-fall accident outside your house. Your lawyer misses the court's filing deadline. As a result you lose the case by default and owe money damages. Because of the court's ruling against you, your credit rating is impaired and you have to back out of various investment plans. You wish to sue the lawyer to get back the interest you would have earned on your investments and the penalties you had to pay for withdrawing from the investment plans.

In addition to showing a direct connection between the misconduct and your loss, most states require that you show that the injury caused a financial loss. It's not good enough to show that you lost an opportunity, or that you experienced minimal or no monetary loss because of the misconduct. You must provide evidence of current financial losses.

Other states lean toward principles of contract law. In those, you need only show that there were slight damages, or that your agreement, whether written or oral, was violated. Proving the contract was broken is enough to give you a right to nominal compensation. (These states also differ on the deadline for filing a lawsuit. See "Defenses" below.)

If you're claiming your lawyer prepared legal documents incompetently, it will often be easy to show how that caused a loss and in what amount. For example, if your lawyer prepared a real estate lease incorrectly, it's fairly easy to attach a dollar value to the loss you suffered.

On the other hand, if you're claiming you lost at trial because your lawyer was incompetent, in most states you will have to prove that you would have won if the lawyer had been competent. This puts the burden on you to prepare for a "trial within the trial"—proving your original case as well as the incompetence. For example, if you're challenging your lawyer's litigation skills or knowledge of the law, in effect you'll have to prove both that the lawyer was guilty of a breach of duty and that your case was solid enough that you would have received more money if not for that breach.

If your case fits this category, be warned: proving two cases can be extremely expensive, and it gives you two chances of losing. Moreover, as discussed in the next section, lawyers often defend themselves by claiming their clients didn't pursue all possible legal avenues to minimize their losses in the original case and therefore don't deserve full compensation.

GETTING COMPENSATED

If you've proven that your lawyer was guilty of malpractice, you have a right to financial reimbursement for your losses. Only the general types of compensation you can collect are listed below. Awards of compensation will depend on the court decisions in your state.

In general, courts will compensate you for the following losses:

Direct Economic Losses. Economic losses are those for which you can show bills, receipts or other financial statements. These can include lost interest, bills for hiring a lawyer to redo the work and payment of back fees for needless or harmful legal work. In addition, you may be entitled to compensation for any financial benefit you would have received if not for the misconduct of your lawyer, including the amount you would have won in court or received if your lawyer had settled the case appropriately.

Foreseeable Losses. Most states allow you to recover any monetary losses your lawyer should have foreseen. For example, you can be compensated for an increase in insurance premiums you had to pay or for the costs of restarting your business if you can show these costs were the result of the malpractice.

Statutory Damages. Some state legislatures have passed laws that supplement the losses you're allowed under court precedents (common law). Typically these provide for nominal damages ($1 or some other small token of "winning"), triple damages in cases of intentional misconduct and the right to collect "extraordinary" damages in cases that involve theft.

Most states will not compensate you for:

Avoidable Losses. Clients have a legal obligation to minimize their losses. Almost every lawyer will attempt to decrease the amount of compensation owed by claiming that the client could have avoided, or mitigated, the losses. One malpractice lawyer we know believes that because the legal system is such a maze of complexities, this defense is particularly inviting in legal malpractice cases.

In one case a court refused to compensate a client for the purchase price of a motel even though the real estate lawyer who negotiated the deal had failed to uncover a mortgage debt that caused the client to lose the property. The court reasoned that the client had had an opportunity to pay off the mortgage to minimize the loss and then sue the lawyer for damages, but had failed to do so.

In practical terms, protecting yourself from this defense usually means hiring still another lawyer to handle the ongoing work on your original legal matter. This way you can prove you are doing everything to "avoid" additional losses. Your malpractice lawyer probably will not agree to handle both cases, because if called as a witness on the status of the original case, that lawyer would then have to withdraw as your malpractice lawyer.

Legal Malpractice Fees. Generally you cannot be reimbursed for your malpractice lawyer's fees. However, try not to confuse the fees you pay for the malpractice suit with the fees you pay to redo the original legal task. You cannot get compensated for the former; you can for the latter.

Emotional Losses. In personal injury cases, the law usually allows you to recover money for such psychological injuries as "pain and suffering" and "mental anguish." Although the law is still evolving in this area, you usually *cannot* get money for these "noneconomic" damages in legal malpractice cases. So even if you can show you suffered severe emotional trauma because your lawyer failed to file your suit within the court's deadline, causing you to lose your case, a court will not compensate you for this "pain and suffering." (In states where you can get compensation for emotional losses, it is based on theories other than negligence and breach of contract. See "Other Theories for Suing" below.)

Speculative Losses. You cannot be compensated for injuries that were not foreseeable or that were caused primarily by something other than your lawyer's misconduct. The causal connection is not considered direct enough. For example, although you could recover for increased auto insurance premiums if your lawyer negligently defended your traffic collision case, you probably could not recover for lost wages even if you are fired because you lost the case. Because the lawyer had no reason to foresee that the misconduct would lead your boss to fire you, the lost wages are considered speculative losses.

Duplicate Compensation. In most states, if you receive compensation from one source—for example, by winning an appeal of your original case or receiving compensation from the lawyer's insurance—you cannot also receive compensation for the same loss directly from the lawyer guilty of misconduct. You would, however, be able to charge the cost of appealing the case to the lawyer who had mishandled it to begin with.

DEFENSES

Even though you prove your lawyer is guilty of malpractice, the lawyer can and will try to reduce the compensation owed. Lawyers will routinely try to prove that the client was partly at fault (contributory negligence), that the client knew the risk of misconduct (assumed the risk) and that the client signed a valid release. These standard defenses, however, are usually unsuccessful in legal malpractice cases.

Lawyers do have at their disposal one effective and often used defense that you should know about:

Statute of Limitations. The only routine defense successfully used in malpractice cases is that your malpractice suit was filed too late, in violation of the statute of limitations. If your lawyer successfully shows you missed the deadline for filing suit, your case will be dismissed by the court.

If your lawyer has any basis to assert a statute of limitations defense, chances are you are headed for complex litigation on the issue. Statute of limitations laws vary from state to state. Typically, they set deadlines that range from one to six years. A very few states have a law that sets a specific statute of limitations for legal malpractice actions. In most states the deadline is based on whether the court characterizes your case as a contract or tort claim. If it's a contract claim, a longer limitation will apply.

Once the deadline is determined, the court must figure out when the clock began to run. Some courts have ruled that it began when the misconduct occurred, others when the injury began, and still others when the lawyer's representation in the matter ended. In some instances, courts have even held that the statute's clock did not begin to run until the client knew or should have known about the injury (called the discovery rule).

OTHER THEORIES FOR SUING

Although the most common theories for suing are negligence and breach of contract, you might be able to sue your
lawyer for intentional misconduct. Intentional misconduct
includes stealing money, lying about the case or misrepre-
senting facts in a way that causes you to lose money. Suits
for intentional lawyer misconduct are no different from
other suits for intentional misconduct and usually are based
on the lawyer's lying about facts to your financial detriment.

If you have good evidence of intentional misconduct, such
as theft, your lawyer is likely to skip town to avoid being
prosecuted by the police and sued by you. If your lawyer
was an uninsured solo practitioner and doesn't have any
property, you are probably out of luck. If your lawyer did
have malpractice insurance or was a member of a law firm,
however, the insurance or the law firm might legally be
required to compensate you for the losses. Be sure you
explore these options for compensation.

CONCLUSION

This book is about a business relationship between two people, an attorney and a client. It lists techniques for avoiding potential problems with the attorney and your options for redress if and when those problems arise. The message of the book is quite simple:

- Take care in hiring.
- Be diligent in managing your case.
- Participate in decisions, but don't hamper your lawyer's ability to give you the expert help you're paying for.
- Keep organized records.
- Don't fire an attorney without thinking about the consequences.
- Be willing to pursue options for redress if the relationship fails.

Most people go to a lawyer for help when they're in trouble. It is hard to be careful and logical in such trying situations, but unless you are, you invite problems that will compound the problems that took you to the lawyer's office in the first place. If you are careful, you may develop an excellent working relationship, but first you must find a lawyer you trust. The benefits are clear: you will get top service for your dollar, have control over your legal affairs, and be more likely to be satisfied both with the result of the lawyer's efforts and the resolution of your legal matter.

It is important to learn as much as you can about your case and the laws involved so that you can be an active participant in making decisions that affect your legal health. The last few years have seen an increase in public awareness about consumers' rights when it comes to legal services. Just as consumers have taken an interest in such areas as automobile safety, they are now learning the importance of knowing and demanding their rights in their dealings with professionals, including lawyers.

It is easy to be intimidated by doctors, lawyers and others we turn to for expert knowledge and skill when we face complex problems. Yet times are changing. In recent years the way consumers receive medical care has undergone a revolution. New emphasis is being placed on preventive health, health education and the medical profession's responsiveness to patients' questions, concerns and decisions.

The same kind of change is happening in the provision of legal services. Consumers are insisting on more control of their legal affairs. More and more legal self-help books and information are available. Legal malpractice claims are increasing in frequency. Consumer groups are challenging the legal profession's monopoly over both the provision and regulation of legal services. Legal consumers are asking lawyers questions and shopping for options in solving legal matters.

This book is intended to help you take advantage of this revolution. Use it to make sure you are fully informed of your rights, involved in decisions about your case, and receiving from your lawyer the expert advice you are buying.

APPENDIXES

MODEL CLIENT–ATTORNEY AGREEMENT

Many attorneys now offer a standard one-page retainer agreement for their clients to sign. The principal reason for this short-form contract is the fear that a longer contract will merely intimidate a potential client. This fear, plus the fact that the primary focus of the document is often the client's agreement to pay, means that these forms are incomplete, especially from the client's point of view.

The following contract was designed to secure the rights and stipulate the responsibilities of both the attorney and client. It is also meant to serve as a basis of discussion through which the client may learn enough about a particular attorney's business practices to make an informed choice as a consumer of legal services.

Whether or not to use this contract or a modified version of it is, of course, a decision to be made by the client and attorney. We have found, however, that most disputes between clients and attorneys could have been avoided if the nature of their relationship had been explicit from the beginning of their relationship.

The following contract is an agreement to employ an attorney on an hourly fee basis. For contingent- or fixed-fee arrangements, replace "Section I, Attorney's Fees" with the appropriate Section I (Contingent or Fixed) that follows the full contract.

CONTRACT TO EMPLOY ATTORNEY

_____ (referred to in this contract as Client) of _____
    (name)   (address)
_____ requests and authorizes _____ (referred to
                                          (name)
in this contract as Attorney) _____ at _____ to
                              (name of firm)   (address)
represent Client as (his/her) Attorney in fact and in law as related
to (specific description of nature and extent of case) (e.g., "a divorce proceeding between X and Y for which Attorney will conduct
negotiations and make court appearances necessary to securing
separation, custody, property and dissolution agreements, including a final decree, but not including an appeal") and against all
additional persons, firms, or corporations who may appear to be
related to this case.

SECTION I

Attorney's Fees

Compensation for Attorney's services shall be based on an hourly
fee arrangement.

(1) Client will pay Attorney the sum of _____ Dollars ($_____)
    per hour for Attorney's time spent in research, writing, consul-
    tation, conference with opposing parties, and other matters
    specifically related to the case described above.
(2) Attorney's additional charges, if any, for appearances in court
    are as follows:
    Routine appearances (e.g., motions for
    continuances) $_____ per _____
    Simple motions (e.g., temporary cus-
    tody, discovery motions, etc.) $_____ per _____
    Trials or hearings $_____ per _____
(3) If a junior partner, associate, or staff attorney within the firm
    performs research or other services for Client, Client will pay
    for those services at the rate of _____ Dollars ($_____) per
    hour. Any court appearance of a junior member of the firm
    will be charged to Client at a rate of _____ percent (_____%)
    of the court appearance charges of Attorney, as given in I (1)
    above.
(4) For all services performed by paralegals for Client, Client will

pay for those services at the rate of _____ Dollars ($_____)
per hour.

(5) If Client is to be charged for secretarial services, Client will
pay for those services at the rate of _____ Dollars ($_____)
per hour.

(6) Time charges will be computed and billed to the tenth of an
hour.

(7) It is necessary to incur certain court costs in order to successfully complete this case. Client agrees to pay for all additional
court costs at the following rates:

- ☐ Filing fees $_____ per _____
- ☐ Deposition fees $_____ per _____
- ☐ Fees for court reporter $_____ per _____
- ☐ Charges for transcripts $_____ per _____
- ☐ Subpoena fees $_____ per _____
- ☐ Fees for expert witnesses $_____ per _____

(8) Attorney estimates that these court costs will not exceed the
sum of _____ Dollars ($_____).

(9) Client also agrees to pay for any of the additional costs
checked below at the following rates:

- ☐ Charges for local phone calls $_____ per _____
- ☐ Charges for postage (e.g., registered
  mail) $_____ per _____
- ☐ Long distance phone charges   _____ % of std. rate
- ☐ Document search and file (including
  computer time) $_____ per _____
- ☐ Special research or investigation
  (e.g., private investigator) $_____ per _____
- ☐ Travel $_____ per _____
- ☐ Other: _____ $_____

(10) Attorney estimates additional costs listed in I(9) will not exceed the sum of _____ Dollars ($_____).

(11) Attorney shall pay all personal and travel expenses incurred
within the (county/city) of _____.

(12) The total estimated number of hours required for the completion of this case are as follows: _____ hours by Attorney; _____
hours by junior members of the firm; and _____ hours by
paralegals.

(13) Attorney estimates that the total cost of fees for the services
of Attorney, junior members and paralegals will not exceed
the sum of _____ Dollars ($_____).

(14) Client will not be liable for any additional costs or fees which exceed the estimates given in I(8), I(10) and I(13) unless Attorney notifies Client of the additional expenses required and receives permission of Client *before* incurring the additional expenses.

(15) (OPTIONAL) The total cost of completing this case shall not under any circumstances exceed the estimates given in I(8), I(10) and I(13) by a factor of _____ percent (_____%).
   [NOTE: For certain cases, there may be several unknown factors at the outset—e.g., whether or not the opposing party will decide to litigate or settle. Therefore, it may be necessary for Attorney and Client to set spending limits conditional on certain events. For example, both "If the case is settled without litigation, the total cost . . ." and "If litigation is required to settle the case . . ." may be necessary.]

SECTION II

Billing Agreement

(1) Client will not be billed for Attorney's time in the preparation or discussion of this employment contract or in discussions concerning disputes over billing. Secretarial time may be charged for the preparation of the original document and copies, the charge to be included in the estimate of additional costs.

(2) Client will pay a retainer of _____ Dollars ($_____) and receive a signed receipt from Attorney for said amount.

(3) Client will receive a statement with detailed itemization of Attorney's, junior members' and paralegals' activities in the case; the amount of time involved; and the additional costs incurred. This statement will be sent to Client on a monthly [or other _____] basis (and/or) per unit of expenditure [e.g., each time the bill increases by $250, an updated statement is to be sent]. If per-unit billing is adopted, that unit will be _____ Dollars ($_____).

(4) All costs and expenses are to be deducted, unless otherwise noted, from the retainer. The current balance of the client's retainer is to be plainly indicated in each itemized statement.

(5) Attorney's fees (may/may not) be deducted from the retainer.

(6) Client is to be notified in writing prior to the depletion of the retainer.

(7) Should the retainer exceed the total cost of completing the case, the remainder is to be returned in full to Client.

(8) Should the cost of conducting the case exceed the retainer but not the estimate or agreed maximum, Client agrees to reimburse Attorney for the additional costs (and/but not) Attorney's fees within _____ days of receipt of an itemized statement.

(9) If the total cost exceeds the retainer but not the agreed maximum, payment for outstanding fees and costs upon completion of the case shall be by (a lump sum payment/payment in full within thirty (30) days of submission of a properly itemized statement/monthly payments of _____ Dollars ($_____)).

(10) Attorney shall receive no other compensation in any manner or form than that provided for expressly by this agreement.

SECTION III

Attorney's Rights and Responsibilities

(1) This contract represents earnest compliance with the Ethical Considerations of the American Bar Association's Code of Professional Responsibility. Attorney consents to be bound by all Canons, Ethical Considerations and Disciplinary Rules of the ABA Code as adopted August 1983 and amended to date.

(2) Violation of any provision within the ABA Code or any agreement within this contract of employment shall be grounds for dismissal of Attorney.

(3) As mandated by the ABA Code, Attorney shall regularly inform Client of progress, if any, in Client's case. This shall include copies of pleadings, briefs, memoranda and relevant correspondence as the case progresses.

(4) Attorney shall freely and frankly discuss the strategy and progress of the case with Client upon request. Attorney must consult and seek permission of Client before taking any action which may significantly affect the outcome or cost of the proceedings.

(5) Attorney may not under any circumstances agree to settle a case without the prior consent of Client.

(6) Withdrawal from representation by Attorney is mandatory upon discharge by Client.

SECTION IV

Client's Rights and Responsibilities

(1) Client agrees to disclose truthfully all relevant information to Attorney upon request.

(2) Client will make (himself/herself) and any documents, persons or things under the Client's control available to Attorney at reasonable times and places for such conferences, inspections, discussions and legal proceedings as may be necessary from time to time.

(3) Client will promptly notify Attorney of any change in Client's address or phone number.

(4) In an effort to increase client participation and to reduce costs, Client will, at the direction of the Attorney, perform these tasks: [e.g., locating evidence, contacting witnesses, filing documents with court clerk, etc. See Chapter 1.]

(5) Failure of Client to seek counsel of Attorney before taking any action which may affect the course or resolution of the case represents sufficient grounds for Attorney withdrawal from employment.

(6) Attorney may not withdraw from employment unless (i) Client receives fourteen (14) days notice prior to withdrawal; (ii) trial is not scheduled within 30 days; (iii) withdrawal will not significantly affect the outcome of imminent proceedings; and (iv) competent counsel can be obtained readily elsewhere by Client.

(7) In the event of withdrawal, Attorney will withdraw in writing and include reasons for withdrawing.

(8) Attorney may not condition completion of representation of Client upon payment of estimated or actual fee under any terms other than those stipulated within this contract.

(9) All documents presented by Client to Attorney remain the exclusive property of Client and must be returned upon demand. Attorney expressly relinquishes all general, possessory or retaining liens known to the common or statutory law.

SECTION V

Disputes

(1) Attorney and Client recognize the benefits of maintaining a harmonious working relationship. Both agree to discuss openly any cause of dissatisfaction and to seek reconciliation. Client will not be billed for this discussion.
(2) Should either party believe itself to be seriously wronged or believe that the terms of this contract have been substantially violated, resolution shall be sought through binding arbitration by a third party mutually agreed to by both Attorney and Client.

SECTION VI

Disclaimer of Warranty

No warranties have been made by Attorney with respect to the successful termination of this case. All expressions made by Attorney about the possible outcome of the case are matters of Attorney's opinion only.

SECTION VII

Power of Attorney

Client grants a power of attorney to Attorney in order that Attorney may execute all documents relevant to the handling of this case, including pleadings, verifications, dismissals, orders and all other documents that Client could otherwise properly execute.

SECTION VIII

Notice

Any notice required under this agreement shall be in writing and shall be deemed to have been duly served if delivered in person, or if delivered at or sent by first class mail to the business address of the person for whom it is intended, as specified in this agreement.

SECTION IX

Law to Govern Contract

The laws of the State of _____ shall govern the construction and interpretation of this agreement.

SECTION X

This contract is valid only with regard to the case described above. An appeal of this case to a higher court, or retrial before a similar court, will require a separate employment contract.

This contract has been read, understood, signed and attested on this day _____, 19__, by the undersigned.

Attorney(s) _____

_____

_____

Client(s) _____

_____

_____

Witness _____

FOR A CONTINGENT-FEE ARRANGEMENT:

SECTION I

Attorney's Fees

Compensation for Attorney's services shall be based on a contingent-fee arrangement.
  (1) The contingent fee shall be based on a percentage of the actual recovery, *after* all expenses indicated in I(3) and (5) have been deducted.
  (2) The contingent fee rate will be _____ percent (_____%).
      (OR)

a. _____ percent (_____%) of the first _____ Dollars ($_____) of the award.

b. _____ percent (_____%) of the next _____ Dollars ($_____) of the award.

c. _____ percent (_____%) of the award that exceeds _____ Dollars ($_____).

(3) It is necessary to incur certain court costs in order to complete this case successfully. Client agrees to pay for all additional court costs at the following rates:

☐ Filing fees $_____ per _____
☐ Deposition fees $_____ per _____
☐ Fees for court reporter $_____ per _____
☐ Charges for transcripts $_____ per _____
☐ Subpoena fees $_____ per _____
☐ Fees for expert witnesses $_____ per _____

(4) Attorney estimates that these court costs will not exceed the sum of _____ Dollars ($_____).

(5) Client also agrees to pay for any of the additional costs checked below at the following rates:

☐ Charges for local phone calls $_____ per _____
☐ Charges for postage (e.g., registered mail) $_____ per _____
☐ Long distance phone charges _____% of std. rate
☐ Document search and file (including computer time) $_____ per _____
☐ Special research or investigation (e.g., private investigator) $_____ per _____
☐ Travel $_____ per _____
☐ Other: _____ $_____ _____

(6) Attorney estimates additional costs listed in I(5) will not exceed the sum of _____ Dollars ($_____).

(7) Attorney shall pay all personal and travel expenses incurred within the (county/city) of _____.

(8) The total estimated additional costs required for the completion of this case are $_____. If the case is settled before a decision of the court, these additional costs will be reduced accordingly.

(9) Client may be requested to advance in part or in full the funds required to meet these costs. If so, this prepayment is designated as the "retainer" in Section II.

(10) Client will not be liable for any additional costs which exceed

the estimate given in I(8) unless Attorney notifies Client of the additional expenses required and receives permission of Client *before* incurring the additional costs.

(11) (OPTIONAL) The total additional costs and expenses incurred in completing this case shall not under any circumstances exceed the estimate given in I(8) by a factor of 20%.

(12) If the case is lost, Client is liable only for the costs incurred, within the limits determined by I(8) and I(11) (if applicable). Client is also liable for opponent's costs, should the court so decide.

(13) The decision to appeal against the verdict of the court is the exclusive right of Client.

(14) Attorney is (given/denied) a special or charging lien on the claim or cause of action, on any sum recovered by way of settlement, and on any judgment that may be recovered, for the sum mentioned above as his/her fee. That is, Client (is/is not) free to use any portion of the recovery for personal purposes until Attorney's fee is paid.

(15) Costs and expenses incurred by Attorney in advancing Client's cause are to be borne by Client. All costs which are not covered by funds advanced by Client to Attorney will be (paid by Client in periodic billings/advanced by Attorney, with reimbursement to be made from the gross proceeds of any recovery, which reimbursements shall be in addition to the percentage fee).

(16) If Client settles the claim without consent of Attorney, Client will pay Attorney a fee computed in accordance with the terms of this agreement and based on the final recovery by Client in the settlement, and Client will reimburse Attorney for all advances made for costs and other expenses.

FOR A FIXED-FEE ARRANGEMENT:

SECTION ONE

Attorney's Fees

Compensation of Attorney's services shall be based on a fixed-fee arrangement.

(1) Client will pay Attorney the sum of _____ Dollars ($_____) as full reimbursement for the completion of all services required to conclude and resolve all aspects of the case described above.

(2) The fixed fee amount given in I(1) does not include any of the additional costs checked below. Client agrees to pay for all additional court costs at the following rates:

☐ Filing fees $_____ per _____
☐ Deposition fees $_____ per _____
☐ Fees for court reporter $_____ per _____
☐ Charges for transcripts $_____ per _____
☐ Subpoena fees $_____ per _____
☐ Fees for expert witnesses $_____ per _____

(3) Attorney estimates that these court costs will not exceed the sum of _____ Dollars ($_____).

(4) Client also agrees to pay for any of the additional costs checked below at the following rates:

☐ Charges for local phone calls $_____ per _____
☐ Charges for postage (e.g., registered mail) $_____ per _____
☐ Long distance phone charges   _____% of std. rate
☐ Document search and file (including computer time) $_____ per _____
☐ Special research or investigation (e.g., private investigator) $_____ per _____
☐ Travel $_____ per _____
☐ Other: _____ $_____

(5) Attorney estimates additional costs listed in I(4) will not exceed the sum of _____ Dollars ($_____).

(6) Attorney shall pay all personal and travel expenses incurred within the (county/city) of _____.

(7) Time charges for any of the additional costs checked above will be computed and billed to the tenth of an hour.

(8) Client will not be liable for any additional costs which exceed the estimate given in I(8) unless Attorney notifies Client of the additional expenses required and receives permission of Client *before* incurring the additional costs.

(10) (OPTIONAL) The total cost of completing this case shall not under any circumstances exceed the sum of _____ Dollars ($_____).

PREPAID LEGAL SERVICES PLAN CONTRACT

This appendix gives the language of an actual prepaid legal services agreement, followed by our plain-language explanation in italics. The agreement includes benefits of a typical "access" plan and was reprinted with permission of the group that offers it, *Montgomery Ward Enterprises Legal Services Plan.*

The information you need about a prepaid legal service plan is *not* usually covered in the form you sign when joining a plan but in the brochures that accompany that form. Most plan brochures are written in plain language, but they also contain a lot of sales talk. They list the free benefits you get by joining the plan as well as the benefits available at reduced rates. Further explanation of some of those benefits is also included in this appendix.

"Montgomery Ward Enterprises is proud to offer . . .

"A new, much needed approach to legal services protection which can immediately benefit you and your family.

"Join this plan and you and your immediate family will be covered for much of the personal and family legal work you would normally expect to require.

"For a monthly fee of only $6.75, you and your family will immediately retain the professional services of a firm of attorneys located near your home or office. The plan attorneys are qualified, in private practice and are licensed by your state."

Montgomery Ward has 2,380 lawyers (680 law firms) participating. To be eligible, they must have been in practice at least three years. According to a plan representative, its lawyers have practiced an average of 13.5 years. However, keep in mind that whether they're qualified to handle your case has more to do with their experience at handling similar problems than the fact that they're licensed. All practicing lawyers have to be "licensed" by the state.

This language also states that you and your immediate family are covered. "Immediate family" includes your spouse and dependents.

"Coverage commences the moment you are enrolled in the Montgomery Ward Enterprises Legal Services Plan.

"IMPORTANT: This enrollment period is limited. Your Enrollment Certificate *must* be received on or before the deadline indicated in order to be eligible. No exceptions will be permitted."

This is an example of a high-pressure sales pitch. Ignore it. If you don't respond "in time," you will probably receive another solicitation later, with a different deadline, or you can call or send in your membership information at any time.

"THE COMPREHENSIVE MONTGOMERY WARD ENTERPRISES LEGAL SERVICES PLAN PROVIDES MUCH OF THE LEGAL SERVICES NORMALLY REQUIRED.

"As a member of the Montgomery Ward Enterprises Legal Services Plan, you will be banding together with thousands of others who will enjoy the benefits of comprehensive legal services.

"In effect, joining the Montgomery Ward Enterprises Legal Services Plan puts a group of experienced, professional attorneys on retainer for you and your family. All you pay is the modest monthly fee of just $6.75.

"The Plan has two parts:

A) Prepaid Benefits *(services covered by your membership fee)*

B) Bonus Benefits *(services not covered but offered at reduced prices)*
"The information on the following pages details your benefits and addresses a number of important questions you may have.

"Please read this material *now.* Remember, this enrollment period is limited. Your Enrollment Certificate *must* be returned on or before the deadline indicated in order to be eligible. No exceptions will be permitted."

Exceptions are the rule here. If they weren't, the plan would go out of business in short order. This sales letter from Montgomery Ward has been seen with a number of different "deadlines" on it, depending on when it was mailed. These aren't true deadlines: they are simply "Buy now!" exhortations.

"PREPAID BENEFITS

"1) UNLIMITED CONSULTATION AND ADVICE BY PHONE OR MAIL
"As soon as we enroll you in the Montgomery Ward Enterprises Legal Services Plan, your plan attorneys will immediately be at your service for consultation and advice during normal business hours concerning any personal or family legal problem you might have. You'll never again have to hesitate about seeking advice from your plan attorneys because you're concerned about cost. Simply call the plan attorneys at the phone number on your membership card and they will be ready to help you."

This states that you can call and get a lawyer as soon as the company processes your check (or gets your credit card number) and sends you a membership card. On that card is the telephone number of the law firm that has been preselected for you. The plan administrator will pick a lawyer from the firm that's nearest you. Each time you call or write, you will get that same law firm. (Other plans use a lawyer "hotline" to take calls. Their members do not get to speak to the same lawyer twice, except by chance.)

The Montgomery Ward plan also includes an "800" number to call if you want an administrator to assign you a different lawyer. Under this plan, you are not given information on a variety of lawyers and then allowed to pick the one you want, but you may later ask to switch if you're not happy with the lawyer picked for you.

Your lawyer is responsible for dealing with all your personal or family legal problems. While most plans provide such free consultation on any legal matter, including criminal matters or litigation problems, you will have to pay extra if you need in-court representation. The lawyers in most plans accept such additional legal work at reduced hourly rates.

The number of times you can call or write your lawyer is unlimited under this plan, as is how long your telephone call can last. However, you must call during "normal" business hours. Ask what's normal for your lawyer. It may be 9 A.M. to 5 P.M. or 7 A.M. to 3 P.M. Under this plan, anyone in your immediate family can call, even your fifteen year-old.

"2) UNLIMITED LEGAL LETTERS AND PHONE CALLS ON YOUR BEHALF

"It could be quite costly, without the Montgomery Ward Enterprises Legal Services Plan, to have an attorney handle legal matters because you would normally be charged hourly rates for your attorney's time. Under the plan, your plan attorneys will make telephone calls and write letters which you both agree are necessary, at no additional charge to you."

Under this plan, your appointed lawyer will handle all the telephone calls and letters you need to resolve your legal problem. The number of such letters and phone calls that can be made for you is unlimited in most states.

To comply with state regulations, however, Arkansas, Indiana, Nebraska and Virginia residents must pay $5 for each letter or phone call a plan lawyer handles for them, and New

*York residents are limited to three letters or phone calls a
year, no more than two of which can be related to the same
matter. Other plans, such as the one offered by Prepaid Legal
Services, allow only one letter or call per problem per year.*

*The Montgomery Ward plan also requires that your lawyer
agree that the letters and calls you want are really necessary
to resolve your problem. If you disagree, the plan administrator may be able to help you and the attorney resolve the
disagreement.*

*It isn't as bad as it may seem, however, because the lawyer
has an incentive to keep you satisfied. Because the lawyer
can be required to handle an unlimited number of calls and
letters for you, it's in the lawyer's interest to resolve the
problem as quickly as possible. Also, the lawyer hopes you
will develop a good working relationship so you will return
for more help on matters that aren't covered by the plan.
After all, that's why the lawyer signed onto the plan in the
first place.*

"3) A SIMPLE PERSONAL WILL FOR YOU AND YOUR IMMEDI-
ATE FAMILY

"As soon as you receive your membership card for the plan,
you can request the preparation of a simple will for you or any
member of your immediate family. Don't worry about cost,
you're totally covered. What's more, if at any time it is necessary to have your will updated, your plan attorneys will attend
to it at no additional charge. This is just one example of the
many benefits you receive as a member of the Montgomery
Ward Enterprises Legal Services Plan."

*This is typical of most plans. It says you and anyone in your
immediate family can get a simple will executed. (In New
York, members and spouses are each entitled to one free will
and annual updates. Arkansas, Nebraska and Virginia residents are charged $15 for this service.)*

*As defined by the plan, a simple will "distributes the prop-
erty generally and does not involve any trusts, complex tax*

considerations or guardianships for minor children." It's important to find out in advance how "simple" a will must be to qualify. Be sure the will you get takes care of your needs. If you want more complex estate planning (e.g., creating a trust for your children or leaving the dining room set to your daughter and the oriental rugs to your son), the "simple will" is not for you. It is only for people who want to leave their property to one person or divide it equally among a number of people. It also does not cover trusts for minors. If you know you need something more complex, you can get it, but at additional cost.

"4) DOCUMENT REVIEW

"Many legal problems are the result of parties entering into undesirable or unfair agreements. You may avoid a potential costly legal dispute by having an attorney examine an agreement before you sign it. Yet, all too often, many citizens fail to do so (and suffer as a consequence) because they are fearful of the expense.

"You need not fret about such costs. Your plan attorneys will review any legal document as long as six pages—leases, real estate papers, installment and rental contracts, promissory notes, bills of sale, powers of attorney, affidavits, and a variety of other legal documents. Cost? You're covered! (If the document is longer than six pages, it will be reviewed at the guaranteed rate of no more than $50 per hour.)"

This plan allows for an unlimited number of legal documents to be reviewed by your plan lawyer during your membership, as long as each document is no longer than six pages. Most plans offer a document-review option and place similar restrictions on it.

Under this plan, you do not need to be named in the document to have it reviewed. For example, you could present a rental agreement for review before signing it. Some plans do require your name to be on any document you ask to have reviewed.

"5) WARRANTY PROBLEMS

"Your plan attorneys will assist you on your warranty problems. They'll write letters and make phone calls on your behalf. And if you have to go to court on the matter, they can
be there to represent you for no more than $50 an hour."

*Both service and product warranties are covered by this
plan. For example, you are promised free advice or help if
you're having a problem with the way a contractor reno-
vated your kitchen or the way a vacuum cleaner operates
before its warranty expires.*

*The other option for dealing with warranty problems, of
course, is to file a complaint with the Better Business Bureau
or a government office of consumer affairs. Both agencies
help resolve these kinds of problems.*

"6) INITIAL FACE-TO-FACE CONSULTATION ON ANY NEW
LEGAL PROBLEM

"When you are confronted by a new legal problem which
can't be handled by telephone or letters, you may consult with
your plan attorneys on a face-to-face basis. You are completely covered on a prepaid basis for any and all such initial
personal consultations."

*This entitles you to one visit to your lawyer's office for each
new problem you have. If you need to discuss the same legal
problem in person more than once, it will cost you $50 an
hour. That rate is a good price in most areas of the country
and a great price in larger metropolitan areas. However, your
plan lawyer will discuss the matter over the telephone as
often as you want, within reason, at no extra charge.*

*Some plans allow unlimited office visits, while others don't
allow even one.*

"7) ADVICE ON SMALL CLAIMS COURT

"If you go to small claims court to settle a grievance, your
plan attorneys will give you advice on how to prepare and
present your case and how to complete necessary forms."

This is true of all plans. The type of help you get on any legal matter depends on the lawyer giving it, however. Some lawyers get a lot of requests for information about small claims court and have prepared written materials on the process for their clients. Others give clients a brief "walk through," and still others offer to help fill out the necessary court papers and discuss presentation styles. The help you can expect depends on the enthusiasm of the lawyer you're assigned to.

Be aware, however, that your lawyer will not go to court with you unless, again, you are willing to pay extra. At $50 an hour, travel, waiting and court time can add up. Get whatever information you can in advance and then handle this kind of claim on your own. In any event, some small claims courts will not allow a lawyer to be in court with you. *

"8) ADVICE ON GOVERNMENT PROGRAMS
"Your plan attorneys will assist you in locating the appropriate government agency to handle your Social Security, Medicare, Veteran's benefits or other matters. Then they'll advise you on how the agency operates, where to go and what benefits you may be entitled to receive."

Again, how much help you get depends on your lawyer. Some lawyers will put you in touch with the right people and give you information that can make collecting benefits a lot less trying. Others may be less acquainted with procedures and will need to fumble through at first. Expect the lawyer to charge extra if you ask to have the benefits collected for you.

"9) $1,000 EMERGENCY BAIL BOND SERVICE
"Should you or any member of your immediate family ever need bail in a hurry, you need only call the 24-hour toll-free

---

*Consult *Small Claims Court: Making Your Way Through the System: A Step-by-Step Guide,* by Theresa Meehan Rudy in association with HALT.

Bail Bond Hot Line phone number and a bail bond of up to $1,000 will be posted as soon as possible."

Depending on the state you live in, a $1,000 bail bond may cover only misdemeanors, traffic offenses and some minor felonies. For example, many judges set bond at $1,000 in shoplifting and speeding cases. For more serious offenses, judges may demand $10,000 bail. Bond companies collect a 10 percent cash deposit for posting your bond.

Before taking advantage of this provision, ask how long you have to reimburse the bond and whether you'll be charged interest. Under this particular plan, you are not charged interest and you have at least 30 days to repay. Bail bond services are not included under the plans offered by either Hyatt or Prepaid Services.

"BONUS BENEFITS

"In addition to your prepaid benefits, the Montgomery Ward Enterprises Legal Services Plan gives you bonus benefits—which provide you with guaranteed maximum fees for six major legal matters, guaranteed rates on contingent fee matters and guaranteed maximum rates on all matters.

GUARANTEED MAXIMUM FEES FOR SIX LEGAL MATTERS

SERVICE	MAXIMUM FEES FOR PLAN MEMBERS
Uncontested Adoption*	$185.00*
Name Change	$155.00
Non-Commercial Real Estate Closing	$175.00
Will with Minor's Trust	$170.00
Non-Support of Spouse or Children	$240.00
Uncontested Divorce**	$210.00**

"*Does not include termination of parental rights.
"**Subject to a limit of net marital assets of $70,000, no children under the age of 18, the defendant spouse is not represented by an attorney and all issues are agreed to without negotiation by the plan attorney."

While the prices for these "simple" legal matters are relatively low compared to those of private lawyers in most places, be aware that many of these matters can be taken care of without a lawyer for even less.

Two quick examples are name changes and uncontested adoptions. To legally change your name in most states, all you need do is file a "name change" form with the appropriate court, then personally notify people and businesses you think should know about your new name. The cost of filing is usually $100 or less. Many uncontested adoptions also never involve a lawyer. Instead, an adoption agency tells the adopting parents what they need to know, including how to prepare for a hearing.

Still, if you don't feel comfortable handling legal matters on your own, these prices are at least better than average. According to a 1988 study by the National Resource Center for Consumers of Legal Services, the national average for real estate closings is $436, for uncontested divorces, $506 and for simple wills, $83.

"MAXIMUM RATES FOR CONTINGENCY FEE CASES

"This is an important benefit. Contingency fee cases occur when you are suing someone for damages such as in personal injury and collection cases. The attorney agrees to being paid a contingency fee, a percentage of any financial recovery, rather than an hourly rate. It is important that you have control on this fee, as it directly impacts the net amount of any settlement or award you may actually receive.

"Attorney contingency fees can go as high as 45%. (In some cases, the fees have been even higher!) You won't have any such worries. Your plan attorneys' percentage is *guaranteed* not to exceed 29% of the recovery if settled before trial, 36% if settled or recovered during or after trial, or 40% if settled or awarded after an appellate brief is prepared. And it may, in fact, be even lower. In matters in which state statutes set the contingent attorney fee, the attorney fee charged will be 10% less than the statutory rate or the attorney's usual fee, whichever is less. For example, in Michigan, personal injury contingency fee rates are limited to 33.3%. There, if an attorney typically charges 33.3%, you would receive the plan rate of 29.9%—a 10% reduction."

This is not much of a discount. Contingency fees, almost always used in personal injury cases, normally run about 30 percent, not 45 percent. If you need to hire a lawyer under this type of arrangement, shop around and see if you can get one to agree to a lower percentage. You may be able to bargain an outside lawyer down from 27 percent, since you already know you're guaranteed that rate by the plan's offer of 10 percent off the lawyer's usual rate.

Under standard "contingency fee" arrangements, if you win, the lawyer gets a percentage of the "take"; if you lose, the lawyer gets expenses but nothing else. The theory is that the lawyer should collect a large slice of the winnings in exchange for the risk of getting nothing, but be assured that any lawyer interested in taking your case is fairly confident of winning. In fact, the more lawyers you find who are interested in your case, the better your chances of bargaining down the percentage fee.

"GUARANTEED RATES ON HOURLY CHARGES!
"On any matter not covered elsewhere, you will pay no more than $50.00 per hour. For instance, after your initial prepaid personal consultation, your plan attorneys will provide you with further personal consultation or represent you in court for no more than $50.00 per hour on matters where no maximum fee is involved.

"This low hourly rate is much lower than many attorneys would charge the general public. Attorneys' hourly rates vary by years of experience, geographic location and other factors. However, one recently published survey reports the median rate that attorneys charge nationally for family law and general personal matters is $75.00 an hour—yet you pay no more than $50.00 an hour when you use Plan Attorneys.

"Plus, remember that your initial personal consultation with your plan attorneys concerning any of these legal problems is already part of your prepaid benefits."

According to the 1988 study by the National Resource Center for Consumers of Legal Services, the average hourly rate for lawyers is between $85 and $90. That makes the $50 hourly rate charged by this plan pretty good, especially when you consider that lawyers in large metropolitan areas charge as high as $150 or $200 an hour. Again, however, before hiring a plan lawyer, explore other options for getting routine legal work done, and shop for a lawyer who has the experience to handle the matter at hand. For instance, a legal clinic may be able to help for less money, or you may be able to do the work on your own with a do-it-yourself publication.

PROCEDURAL STAGES OF A LAWSUIT

$\mathbf{T}$he following flow chart depicts the stages of a typical civil lawsuit. (Criminal lawsuits have different procedures.) This description is general and, because each state and the federal court system has its own procedures, you will have to look at a specific practice and procedure book for items such as the names of documents.

Procedural Stages of a Lawsuit: Discovery

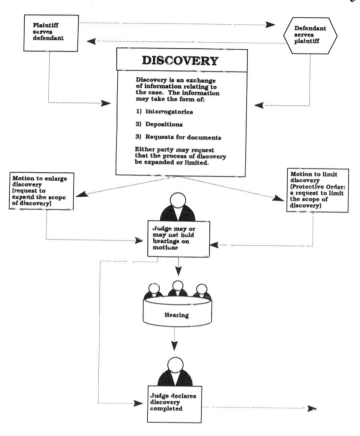

Procedural Stages of a Lawsuit: Pleading

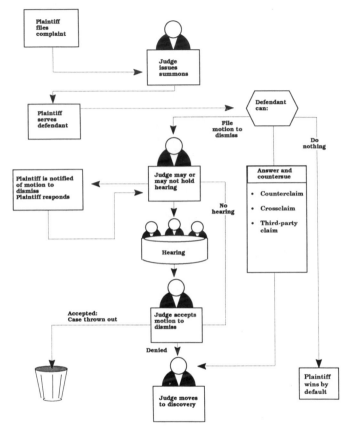

Procedural Stages of a Lawsuit: Pre-Trial

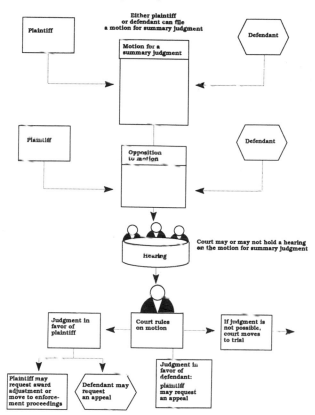

Procedural Stages of a Lawsuit: Trial

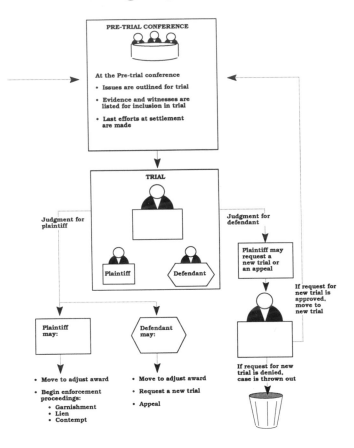

PRE-TRIAL CONFERENCE

At the Pre-trial conference

- Issues are outlined for trial

- Evidence and witnesses are listed for inclusion in trial

- Last efforts at settlement are made

TRIAL

Judgment for plaintiff

Judgment for defendant

Plaintiff

Defendant

Plaintiff may request a new trial or an appeal

If request for new trial is approved, move to new trial

Plaintiff may:

Defendant may:

If request for new trial is denied, case is thrown out

- Move to adjust award

- Begin enforcement proceedings:
  - Garnishment
  - Lien
  - Contempt

- Move to adjust award

- Request a new trial

- Appeal

APPENDIX **IV**

STATE BAR PROGRAMS FOR RESOLVING COMPLAINTS AGAINST LAWYERS

This appendix lists addresses and phone numbers for grievance committees, client security trust fund offices and fee arbitration programs for all fifty states, the District of Columbia, the Virgin Islands and Puerto Rico.

Where state offices handle the matter, that office is listed. If the issue is handled at a local office, either that office is listed or we suggest you contact the state office for a local referral.

All information is accurate as of November 1989. Data on grievance committees and client security trust fund offices were compiled by the American Bar Association and data on fee arbitration programs were compiled by HALT. Because the names and addresses of state agencies may change at any time, you should verify the information with your state bar or the American Bar Association.

ALABAMA

Attorney Grievance
State Office:
General Counsel
Alabama State Bar
Center for Professional Responsibility
1019 S. Perry St.
Montgomery, AL 36104
(205) 269-1515

Client Security Trust Fund
Executive Director
Alabama State Bar
P.O. Box 671
415 Dexter St.
Montgomery, AL 36101
(205) 269-1515

Fee Arbitration
No statewide program; state bar refers cases to local fee arbitration where available.
(Address, telephone same as for Client Security Trust Fund.)

ALASKA

Attorney Grievance
State Office:
Bar Counsel
Alaska Bar Association
P.O. Box 100279
Anchorage, AK 99510
(907) 272-7469

Client Security Trust Fund
Assistant Bar Counsel
(Address, telephone same as for Attorney Grievance.)

Fee Arbitration
Fee Arbitration Committee
(Address, telephone same as for Attorney Grievance.)

ARIZONA

Attorney Grievance
State Office:
Chief Bar Counsel
State Bar of Arizona
363 N. First Ave.
Phoenix, AZ 85003-1580
(602) 252-4804, ext. 225

Client Security Trust Fund
Chief Bar Counsel
(Address, telephone same as for Attorney Grievance.)

Fee Arbitration
Committee on Arbitration of Fee Disputes
(Address, telephone same as for Attorney Grievance.)

ARKANSAS

Attorney Grievance
State Office:
Supreme Court of Arkansas
Committee on Professional Conduct
364 Prospect Bldg.
1501 N. University
Little Rock, AR 72207
(501) 664-8658

Client Security Trust Fund
Clerk
Arkansas Supreme Court Justice Bldg.
625 Marshall St.

Little Rock, AR 72201
(501) 682-6849

Fee Arbitration
None.

CALIFORNIA

Attorney Grievance
Southern California:
Chief Trial Counsel
Intake/Legal Advice
State Bar of California
333 S. Beaudry Ave., 9th Floor
Los Angeles, CA 90017
(213) 580-5000
(800) 843-9053 (California residents only)

Northern California:
Chief Trial Counsel
State Bar of California
555 Franklin St.
San Francisco, CA 94102
(415) 561-8200
(use toll-free number above)

Client Security Trust Fund
Southern California Grievance Committee district office handles all cases.
(Address same as for Southern California Grievance Committee.)
(213) 580-5140

Fee Arbitration
Mandatory Fee Arbitration
(Address, telephone same as for Northern California Grievance Committee)

COLORADO

Attorney Grievance
State Office:
Disciplinary Counsel
Supreme Court of Colorado
600 17th St., Suite 510 S.
Dominion Plaza Bldg.
Denver, CO 80202
(303) 893-8121

Client Security Trust Fund
Executive Director
Colorado Bar Association
1900 Grant St., Suite 950
Denver, CO 80203-4309
(303) 860-1112

Fee Arbitration
Legal Fee Arbitration Committee
(Address, telephone same as for Client Security Trust Fund.)

CONNECTICUT

Attorney Grievance
State Office:
Statewide Bar Counsel
P.O. Box 6888, Station A
Hartford, CT 06106
(203) 247-6264

Client Security Trust Fund
Assistant Executive Director
Connecticut Bar Association
101 Corporate Place
Rocky Hill, CT 06067
(203) 721-0025

Fee Arbitration
Committee on Arbitration of Fee Disputes
(Address, telephone same as for Client Security Trust Fund.)

DELAWARE

Attorney Grievance
State Office:
Disciplinary Counsel
Board on Professional Respon-
sibility of the Supreme Court of
Delaware
831 Tatnall St.
P.O. Box 1808
Wilmington, DE 19899
(302) 571-8703

Client Security Trust Fund
Administrator
Delaware State Bar Association
706 Market St.
Wilmington, DE 19801
(302) 658-5278

Fee Arbitration
Fee Dispute Conciliation and
Mediation Committee
(Address, telephone same as for
Client Security Trust Fund.)

DISTRICT OF COLUMBIA

Attorney Grievance
District Office:
Bar Counsel
District of Columbia Bar
Bldg. A, Room 127
515 5th St. NW
Washington, DC 20001
(202) 638-1501

Client Security Trust Fund
Assistant Executive Director
District of Columbia Bar
1707 L St. NW, 6th Floor
Washington, DC 20036
(202) 331-3883

Fee Arbitration
Attorney-Client Arbitration
Board
(Address, telephone same as for
Client Security Trust Fund.)

FLORIDA

Attorney Grievance
State Office:
Staff Counsel
Florida Bar
650 Apalachee Pkwy.
Tallahassee, FL 32399-2300
(800) 874-0005 (out of state)
(800) 342-8060 (Florida residents only)
(904) 561-5839

Client Security Trust Fund
Programs Division
(Address same as for
Attorney Grievance.)
(904) 561-5600

Fee Arbitration
Fee Arbitration Committee
(Address, telephone same as for
Attorney Grievance.)

GEORGIA

Attorney Grievance
State Office:
General Counsel
State Bar of Georgia
50 Hurt Plaza, Suite 800
Atlanta, GA 30303
(404) 527-8720

Client Security Trust Fund
Assistant General Counsel
(Address, telephone same as for
Attorney Grievance.)

Fee Arbitration
Committee on Arbitration of
Fee Disputes
(Address, telephone same as for
Attorney Grievance.)

HAWAII

Attorney Grievance
State Office:
Chief Disciplinary Counsel
Office of Disciplinary Counsel
Supreme Court of the State of
Hawaii
1164 Bishop St., Suite 600
Honolulu, HI 96813
(808) 521-4591

Client Security Trust Fund
Hawaii Supreme Court Clerk
P.O. Box 2560
Honolulu, HI 96804
(808) 599-8938

Fee Arbitration
Attorney-Client Coordination
Committee
Hawaii State Bar Association
P.O. Box 26
Honolulu, HI 96810
(808) 537-1868

IDAHO

Attorney Grievance
State Office:
Bar Counsel
Idaho State Bar
P.O. Box 895
204 W. State St.
Boise, ID 83701
(208) 342-8958

Client Security Trust Fund
Executive Director
(Address, telephone same as for
Attorney Grievance.)

Fee Arbitration
Fee Arbitration Program
(Address, telephone same as for
Attorney Grievance.)

ILLINOIS

Attorney Grievance
Chicago and Northern Illinois:
Attorney Registration and Disciplinary Commission of the Supreme Court of Illinois
203 N. Wabash Ave., Suite 1900
Chicago, IL 60601-2474
(312) 346-0690
(800) 826-8625 (Illinois residents only)

Central and Southern Illinois:
Attorney Registration and Disciplinary Commission of the Supreme Court of Illinois
One N. Old Capitol Plaza, Suite 330
Springfield, IL 62701-1507
(217) 522-6838
(800) 252-8048 (Illinois residents only)

Client Security Trust Fund
Clients' Security Trust Fund of
the Bar of Illinois
Illinois Bar Center
Springfield, IL 62701
(217) 525-1760

Fee Arbitration
Voluntary Fee Arbitration
(Address, telephone same as for
Client Security Trust Fund.)

INDIANA

Attorney Grievance
State Office:
Executive Secretary
Disciplinary Commission of the
Supreme Court of Indiana
628 I.S.T.A. Bldg., Room 814
150 W. Market St.
Indianapolis, IN 46204
(317) 232-1807

Client Security Trust Fund
Assistant Executive Director
Indiana Bar Center
Indiana State Bar Association
230 E. Ohio St., 4th Floor
Indianapolis, IN 46204
(317) 639-5465

Fee Arbitration
No statewide program; state bar
refers cases to local fee arbitra-
tion where available.
(Address, telephone same as for
Client Security Trust Fund.)

IOWA

Attorney Grievance
State Office:
Ethics Administrator
Iowa State Bar Association
1101 Fleming Bldg.
Des Moines, IA 50309
(515) 243-3179

Client Security Trust Fund
Assistant Court Administrator
Clients' Security Trust Fund
State Capitol
Des Moines, IA 50319
(515) 281-3718

Fee Arbitration
No statewide program; state bar
refers cases to local fee arbitra-
tion where available.
(Address, telephone same as for
Attorney Grievance.)

KANSAS

Attorney Grievance
State Office:
Disciplinary Administrator
Supreme Court of Kansas
Kansas Judicial Center, Room
278
301 W. 10th St.
Topeka, KS 66612
(913) 296-2486

Client Security Trust Fund
Executive Director
Kansas Bar Association
1200 Harrison St.
P.O. Box 1037
Topeka, KS 66601
(913) 234-5696

Fee Arbitration
No statewide program; state bar
refers cases to local fee arbitra-
tion where available.
(Address, telephone same as for
Client Security Trust Fund.)

KENTUCKY

Attorney Grievance
State Office:
Bar Counsel
Kentucky Bar Association
W. Main at Kentucky River
Frankfort, KY 40601
(502) 564-3795

Client Security Trust Fund
(Address, telephone same as for Attorney Grievance.)

Fee Arbitration
Legal Fee Arbitration Plan
(Address, telephone same as for Attorney Grievance.)

LOUISIANA

Attorney Grievance
State Office:
Executive Counsel
Louisiana State Bar Association
601 St. Charles Ave.
New Orleans, LA 70130
(504) 566-1600

Client Security Trust Fund
Executive Counsel
(Address, telephone same as for Attorney Grievance.)

Fee Arbitration
None.

MAINE

Attorney Grievance
State Office:
Bar Counsel
Maine Board of Overseers of the Bar
P.O. Box 1820

Augusta, ME 04332-1820
(207) 623-1121

Client Security Trust Fund
None.

Fee Arbitration
Fee Arbitration Commission
(Address, telephone same as for Attorney Grievance.)

MARYLAND

Attorney Grievance
State Office:
Bar Counsel
Attorney Grievance Commission of Maryland
District Court Bldg.
580 Taylor Ave., Room 404
Annapolis, MD 21401
(301) 974-2791

Client Security Trust Fund
Administrator
108 W. Circle Ave., Room 213
Salisbury, MD 21801
(301) 543-8410

Fee Arbitration
Committee on Resolution of Fee Disputes
(Address, telephone same as for Client Security Trust Fund.)

MASSACHUSETTS

Attorney Grievance
State Office:
Bar Counsel
Massachusetts Board of Bar Overseers
11 Beacon St.
Boston, MA 02108
(617) 720-0700

Client Security Trust Fund
Board Counsel
(Address, telephone same as for
Attorney Grievance.)

Fee Arbitration
Fee Arbitration Board
Massachusetts Bar Association
20 West St.
Boston, MA 02111
(617) 542-3602

MICHIGAN

Attorney Grievance
State Office:
Deputy Grievance Administrator
Michigan Attorney Grievance
Commission
Marquette Bldg., Suite 600
243 W. Congress
Detroit, MI 48226
(313) 965-6585

Client Security Trust Fund
State Bar of Michigan
306 Townsend St.
Lansing, MI 48933-2083
(517) 372-9030, ext. 3010

Fee Arbitration
Fee Arbitration Program
(Address, telephone same as for
Attorney Grievance.)

MINNESOTA

Attorney Grievance
State Office:
Director
Office of Lawyers' Professional
Responsibility

520 Lafayette Rd., 1st Floor
St. Paul, MN 55155-4196
(612) 296-3952

Client Security Trust Fund
Director
(Address, telephone same as for
Attorney Grievance.)

Fee Arbitration
No statewide program; disciplinary committee refers cases
to local fee arbitration where
available.
(Address, telephone same as for
Attorney Grievance.)

MISSISSIPPI

Attorney Grievance
State Office:
General Counsel
Mississippi State Bar
P.O. Box 2168
Jackson, MS 39225-2168
(601) 948-4471

Client Security Trust Fund
Assistant General Counsel
(Address, telephone same as for
Attorney Grievance.)

Fee Arbitration
Resolution of Fee Disputes
Committee
(Address, telephone same as for
Attorney Grievance.)

MISSOURI

Attorney Grievance
State Office:
General Chair
Missouri Bar Administration

P.O. Box 349
Sedalia, MO 65301
(816) 826-7890

Client Security Trust Fund
Director of Programs
Missouri Bar
P.O. Box 119
Jefferson City, MO 65102
(314) 635-4128

Fee Arbitration
No statewide program; state bar
refers cases to local fee arbitra-
tion where available.
(Address, telephone same as for
Attorney Grievance.)

MONTANA

Attorney Grievance
State Office:
Administrative Secretary
Commission on Practice of the
Supreme Court of Montana
Justice Bldg., Room 315
215 N. Sanders
Helena, MT 59620
(406) 444-2608

Client Security Trust Fund
Executive Director
State Bar of Montana
P.O. Box 577
Helena, MT 59624
(406) 442-7660

Fee Arbitration
Voluntary Fee Arbitration
(Address, telephone same as for
Client Security Trust Fund.)

NEBRASKA

Attorney Grievance
State Office:
Counsel for Discipline
Nebraska State Bar Association
P.O. Box 81809
Lincoln, NE 68501
(402) 475-7091

Client Security Trust Fund
Executive Director
Nebraska State Bar Association
635 S. 14th St.
Lincoln, NE 68508
(402) 475-7091

Fee Arbitration
None.

NEVADA

Attorney Grievance
State Office:
Bar Counsel
State Bar of Nevada
500 S. 3rd St., Suite 2
Las Vegas, NV 89101
(702) 382-0502

Client Security Trust Fund
Staff Administrator
State Bar of Nevada
P.O. Box 2229
Reno, NV 89505
(702) 329-1766

Fee Arbitration
Fee Arbitration Program
(Address, telephone same as for
Attorney Grievance.)

NEW HAMPSHIRE

Attorney Grievance
State Office:
Administrator
New Hampshire Supreme Court
Professional Conduct Committee
18 N. Main St., Suite 205
Concord, NH 03301
(603) 224-5828

Client Security Trust Fund
Staff Liaison
Clients' Indemnity Fund
New Hampshire Bar Association
18 Centre St.
Concord, NH 03301
(603) 224-6942

Fee Arbitration
Fee Dispute Resolution Committee
(Address, telephone same as for
Client Security Trust Fund.)

NEW JERSEY

Attorney Grievance
State Office:
Director, Office of Attorney Ethics
Supreme Court of New Jersey
Richard J. Hughes Justice Complex, CN-963
Trenton, NJ 08625
(609) 292-8750

Client Security Trust Fund
Director and Counsel
(Address, telephone same as for
Attorney Grievance, except CN-961)
(609) 984-7179

Fee Arbitration
District Fee Arbitration Committee
(Address, telephone same as for
Attorney Grievance.)

NEW MEXICO

Attorney Grievance
State Office:
Chief Disciplinary Counsel
Disciplinary Board of the Supreme Court of New Mexico
400 Gold SW, Suite 712
Albuquerque, NM 87102
(505) 842-5781

Client Security Trust Fund
None.

Fee Arbitration
Fee Arbitration Committee
State Bar of New Mexico
P.O. Box 25883
Albuquerque, NM 87125
(505) 842-6132

NEW YORK

Attorney Grievance
New York City (First Dept.):
Chief Counsel
Departmental Disciplinary
Committee for the First Judicial
Department
41 Madison Ave., 39th Floor
New York, NY 10010
(212) 685-1000

New York City (Second Dept.):
Chief Counsel
State of New York Grievance
Committee for the 2nd and 11th
Judicial Districts

Municipal Bldg., 12th Floor
210 Joralemon St.
Brooklyn, NY 11201
(718) 624-7851

New York State (Second Dept.):
Chief Counsel
Grievance Committee for the
9th Judicial District
Crosswest Office Center
399 Knollwood Rd., Suite 200
White Plains, NY 10603
(914) 949-4540

New York State (Second Dept.):
Chief Counsel
New York State Grievance Committee for the 10th Judicial District
900 Ellison Ave., Room 304
Westbury, NY 11590
(516) 832-8585

New York State (Third Dept.):
Chief Attorney
3rd Department Committee on
Professional Standards
Alfred E. Smith State Office
Bldg., 22nd Floor
P.O. Box 7013, Capitol Station
Annex
Albany, NY 12225-0013
(518) 474-8816

New York State (Fourth Dept.):
Chief Attorney
Appellate Division, Supreme
Court
4th Judicial Department
Office of Grievance Committee
1036 Ellicott Square Bldg.

Buffalo, NY 14203
(716) 855-1191

Client Security Trust Fund
Executive Director
Clients' Security Trust Fund of
the State of New York
55 Elk St.
Albany, NY 12210
(518) 474-8438

Fee Arbitration
No statewide program; state bar
refers cases to local fee arbitration where available.
New York State Bar
1 Elk St.
Albany, NY 12207
(518) 463-3200

NORTH CAROLINA

Attorney Grievance
State Office:
Counsel
North Carolina State Bar
208 Fayetteville St. Mall
P.O. Box 25908
Raleigh, NC 27611
(919) 828-4620

Client Security Trust Fund
Executive Director
(Address, telephone same as for
Attorney Grievance.)

Fee Arbitration
No statewide program; state bar
refers cases to local fee arbitration where available.
(Address, telephone same as for
Attorney Grievance.)

NORTH DAKOTA

Attorney Grievance
State Office:
Disciplinary Counsel
Disciplinary Board of the Supreme Court
P.O. Box 2297
Bismarck, ND 58502
(701) 224-3348

Client Security Trust Fund
Staff Administrator
State Bar Association of North Dakota
P.O. Box 2136
Bismarck, ND 58502
(701) 255-1404

Fee Arbitration
Fee Arbitration Committee
(Address, telephone same as for Client Security Trust Fund.)

OHIO

Attorney Grievance
State Office:
Disciplinary Counsel
Office of Disciplinary Counsel of the Supreme Court of Ohio
175 S. 3rd St., Suite 280
Columbus, OH 43215
(614) 461-0256

Summit County:
Executive Director
Akron Bar Association
90 S. High St.
Akron, OH 44308
(216) 253-5007

Hamilton County:
Bar Counsel
Cincinnati Bar Association
35 E. 7th St., Suite 800
Cincinnati, OH 45202-2411
(513) 381-8213

Cuyahoga County:
Counsel
Cleveland Bar Association
113 St. Clair Ave. NE, 2nd Floor
Cleveland, OH 44114-1253
(216) 696-3525

Franklin County:
Bar Counsel
Columbus Bar Association
40 S. Third St.
Columbus, OH 43215
(614) 221-4112

Montgomery County:
Executive Director
Dayton Bar Association
1700 Hulman Bldg.
Dayton, OH 45402-1671
(513) 222-7902

Lucas County:
Executive Director
Toledo Bar Association
311 N. Superior St.
Toledo, OH 43604
(419) 242-9363

Client Security Trust Fund
Clients' Security Trust Fund of Ohio
Rhodes State Office Tower
30 E. Broad St., 23rd Floor
Columbus, OH 43266-0419
(614) 644-1700

Fee Arbitration
No statewide program; state bar refers cases to local fee arbitration where available.
Ohio State Bar Association
33 W. 11th Ave,
Columbus, OH 43201-2099
(614) 421-2121

OKLAHOMA

Attorney Grievance
State Office:
General Counsel
Oklahoma Bar Center
1901 N. Lincoln Blvd.
P.O. Box 53036
Oklahoma City, OK 73152
(405) 524-2365

Client Security Trust Fund
Executive Director
(Address, telephone same as for Attorney Grievance.)

Fee Arbitration
No statewide program; state bar refers cases to local fee arbitration where available.
(Address, telephone same as for Attorney Grievance.)

OREGON

Attorney Grievance
State Office:
Disciplinary Counsel
Oregon State Bar
P.O. Box 1689
Lake Oswego, OR 97035-0889
(503) 620-0222

Client Security Trust Fund
Staff Liaison
Oregon State Bar
5200 SW Meadows Rd.
P.O. Box 1689
Lake Oswego, OR 97035-0889
(503) 620-0222, ext. 320

Fee Arbitration
Fee Arbitration Committee
(Address, telephone same as for Attorney Grievance.)

PENNSYLVANIA

Attorney Grievance
State Office:
Chief Disciplinary Counsel
Disciplinary Board of the Supreme Court of Pennsylvania
2100 N. American Building
121 S. Broad St.
Philadelphia, PA 19107
(215) 560-6296

Client Security Trust Fund
Executive Director
Pennsylvania Client Security Trust Fund
1515 Market St., Suite 1420
Philadelphia, PA 19102
(215) 560-6335

Fee Arbitration
No statewide program; disciplinary board refers cases to local fee arbitration where available.
(Address same as for Attorney Grievance.)
(717) 238-6715

PUERTO RICO

Attorney Grievance
Presidente
Comisión de Ética Profesional
Colegio de Abogados de Puerto Rico
Apartado 1900
San Juan, PR 00903
(809) 721-3358

Secretary
Tribunal Supremo de Puerto Rico
Apartado 2392
San Juan, PR 00903
(809) 723-6033

Solicitor General
Departmento de Justicia
Apartado 192
San Juan, PR 00902
(809) 721-2924

Client Security Trust Fund
None.

Fee Arbitration
None.

RHODE ISLAND

Attorney Grievance
State Office:
Chief Disciplinary Counsel
Disciplinary Board of the Supreme Court of Rhode Island
Supreme Court Bldg.
250 Benefit St., 9th Floor
Providence, RI 02903
(401) 277-3270

Client Security Trust Fund
Executive Director
Rhode Island Bar Association

91 Friendship St.
Providence, RI 02903
(401) 421-5740

Fee Arbitration
Fee Arbitration Committee
(Address, telephone same as for Attorney Grievance.)

SOUTH CAROLINA

Attorney Grievance
State Office:
Administrative Assistant
Board of Commissioners on Grievances and Discipline
P.O. Box 11330
Columbia, SC 29211
(803) 734-2038

Client Security Trust Fund
Director of Public Services
South Carolina Bar
950 Taylor St.
P.O. Box 608
Columbia, SC 29202
(803) 799-6653

Fee Arbitration
Resolution of Fee Disputes Board
(Address, telephone same as for Client Security Trust Fund.)

SOUTH DAKOTA

Attorney Grievance
State Office:
Investigator
Disciplinary Board of the State Bar of South Dakota
P.O. Box 476
Tyndall, SD 57066
(605) 589-3333

Client Security Trust Fund

Executive Director
State Bar of South Dakota
222 E. Capitol
Pierre, SD 57501
(605) 224-7554

Fee Arbitration

None.

TENNESSEE

Attorney Grievance

State Office:
Chief Disciplinary Counsel
Board of Professional Responsibility of the Supreme Court of Tennessee
1105 Kermit Dr., Suite 730
Nashville, TN 37217
(615) 361-7500

Client Security Trust Fund

None.

Fee Arbitration

No statewide program; state bar refers cases to local fee arbitration where available.
(Address, telephone same as for Client Security Trust Fund.)

TEXAS

Attorney Grievance

State Office:
General Counsel
State Bar of Texas
P.O. Box 12487
Capitol Station
Austin, TX 78711
(512) 463-1391

Client Security Trust Fund

General Counsel's Office
(Address same as for Attorney Grievance.)
(512) 475-6202

Fee Arbitration

No statewide program; state bar refers cases to local fee arbitration where available.
(Address, telephone same as for Attorney Grievance.)

UTAH

Attorney Grievance

State Office:
Bar Counsel
Utah State Bar
645 S. 200 East
Salt Lake City, UT 84111-3834
(801) 531-9110

Client Security Trust Fund

Executive Director
(Address same as for Attorney Grievance.)
(801) 531-9077

Fee Arbitration

Fee Arbitration Committee
(Address, telephone same as for Attorney Grievance.)

VERMONT

Attorney Grievance

State Office:
Professional Conduct Board
16 High St.
P.O. Box 801
Brattleboro, VT 05301
(802) 254-2345

Client Security Trust Fund
Staff Administrator
Vermont Bar Association
P.O. Box 100
Montpelier, VT 05602
(802) 223-2020

Fee Arbitration
Arbitration of Fee Complaints
Committee
(Address, telephone same as for
Client Security Trust Fund.)

VIRGINIA

Attorney Grievance
State Office:
Bar Counsel
Virginia State Bar
801 E. Main St., 10th Floor
Richmond, VA 23219
(804) 786-3140

Client Security Trust Fund
Staff Administrator
(Address, telephone same as for
Attorney Grievance.)
(804) 786-2061

Fee Arbitration
No statewide program; state bar
refers cases to local fee arbitra-
tion where available.
(Address, telephone same as for
Attorney Grievance.)

VIRGIN ISLANDS

Attorney Grievance
Chair
Ethics and Grievance Commit-
tee

U.S. Virgin Islands Bar Association
P.O. Box 6520
St. Thomas, VI 00801
(809) 774-6490

Client Security Trust Fund
None.

Fee Arbitration
None.

WASHINGTON

Attorney Grievance
State Office:
Chief Disciplinary Counsel
Washington State Bar Association
500 Westin Bldg.
2001 6th Ave.
Seattle, WA 98121-2599
(206) 448-0307

Client Security Trust Fund
General Counsel
(Address, telephone same as for
Attorney Grievance.)

Fee Arbitration
Fee Arbitration Committee
(Address, telephone same as for
Attorney Grievance.)

WEST VIRGINIA

Attorney Grievance
State Office:
Bar Counsel
West Virginia State Bar
State Capitol
2006 Canawha Blvd.
Charleston, WV 25301
(304) 348-2456

Client Security Trust Fund
Staff Administrator
(Address, telephone same as for
Attorney Grievance.)

Fee Arbitration
None.

WISCONSIN

Attorney Grievance
State Office:
Administrator
Board of Attorneys Professional
Responsibility
Supreme Court of Wisconsin
Tenney Bldg.
110 E. Main St., Room 410
Madison, WI 53703
(608) 267-7274

Client Security Trust Fund
Legal Services Assistant
State Bar of Wisconsin
P.O. Box 7158
Madison, WI 53707
(608) 257-3838

Fee Arbitration
Committee on Resolution of Fee
Disputes
(Address, telephone same as for
Client Security Trust Fund.)

WYOMING

Attorney Grievance
State Office:
Bar Counsel
Wyoming State Bar
P.O. Box 109
Cheyenne, WY 82003-0109
(307) 632-9061

Client Security Trust Fund
Executive Secretary
(Address, telephone same as for
Attorney Grievance.)

Fee Arbitration
Committee on Resolution of Fee
Disputes
(Address, telephone same as for
Attorney Grievance.)

GLOSSARY OF TERMS

The following terms are used in this book and in litigation generally. Italicized terms in definitions are themselves defined in other entries.

Admonition   See *Reprimand.*

Affidavit   Written statement of fact voluntarily signed and sworn to before a person who has authority to administer an oath; it can be used in court as evidence.

Answer   *Defendant*'s formal written statement of defense against the *plaintiff*'s complaint in a lawsuit. The answer addresses the truth or falsity of the plaintiff's claims and can include a *counterclaim.*

Appeal   Request that a higher court review the decision of a lower court to correct errors in the application of law or procedure.

Appellant   Person who initiates an *appeal.*

Arbitration   Method of settling disputes in which the two sides submit arguments to a neutral third party or panel, which makes a decision after listening to both sides and considering the evidence.

Attorney discipline   Act by a state bar grievance committee or court sanctioning a lawyer for violating the state's *code of professional responsibility.*

Breach of contract   Reason for suing based on failure to live up to a legally binding promise, such as the terms of a client-attorney agreement.

Brief   Written statement prepared by one side in a lawsuit to explain to a judge the essential facts of a case and the applicable law.

Censure See *Reprimand.*

Client Security Trust Fund State bar program in which money collected from attorneys is used to reimburse victims of lawyer theft.

Code of professional responsibility Rules that govern a lawyer's right to practice law in a state. A lawyer's license can be removed or suspended, or the lawyer can be reprimanded, for violating the code. Each state's code is based on the American Bar Association's model code.

Comingling Lawyer misuse of a client's funds by mingling them with the lawyer's personal money. This is a violation of every state's *code of professional responsibility.*

Common law Law derived by U.S. courts from early English court decisions, not from legislative enactment or constitutional provisions.

Complaint Document that officially initiates a lawsuit. It includes, among other things, a statement of the facts and allegation of the wrong or harm done to the one making the complaint (*plaintiff*) by the other side (*defendant*); a request for help from the court; and an explanation of why the court has the power to comply with that request.

Conflict of interest Attorney's association or tie that would jeopardize or bias representation of the client. Failing to disclose a potential conflict of interest to a client is a violation of every state's *code of professional responsibility.*

Contempt Willful disobedience of a judge's command or an official court order, punishable by fine or imprisonment.

Contingency fee Attorney's fee based on a percentage of the amount awarded to the client. If no amount is awarded, no fee must be paid, although the client will be required to pay legal expenses.

Continuance Postponement of a legal proceeding.

Counter-claim Claim made by a *defendant* in a civil lawsuit that, in effect, sues the *plaintiff.*

Damages Amount of money or other relief requested by the *plaintiff* in a lawsuit.

Default judgment Decision in favor of the *plaintiff* because the *defendant* failed to file a response to the plaintiff's *complaint* within the time required by law, or failed to appear in court on the scheduled date of the hearing or trial.

Defendant Person against whom a legal action is filed.

Deposition   Out-of-court process of taking the sworn testimony of a witness. This is usually done by a lawyer with a lawyer from the other side being permitted to attend or participate. The purpose is to disclose relevant information so that each side can evaluate its case before going to trial and decide whether to pursue the claim or settle out of court.

Disbarment   Removing a lawyer's license to practice in a state for violating that state's *code of professional responsibility*. This is the most severe form of *attorney discipline*. In most states a lawyer may reapply for admission to practice five years after being disbarred.

Disciplinary agency   State agency that processes *complaints* against lawyers to determine if the *code of professional responsibility* has been violated sufficiently to warrant *attorney discipline*. Also called *grievance committee*.

Discovery   Before-trial formal and informal exchange of information between the sides in a lawsuit. Two types of discovery are *interrogatories* and *depositions*.

Discovery rule   One of three possible rules states may use to set a deadline or *statute of limitations* for filing a malpractice lawsuit. States that use the discovery rule hold that the *statute of limitations* "clock" does not begin to run until the client knows or should know that the injury has occurred.

Economic loss   Damages a *plaintiff* can demonstrate with bills, receipts, or other financial statements.

Expenses   Charges for a lawyer's work other than fees, typically including long distance telephone charges, photocopying, court filing fees and expert witness fees.

Fee arbitration   Out-of-court forum for settling fee disputes between attorneys and clients. Many state and local bar associations have established fee arbitration committees.

Flat fee   Lawyer's fee based on a fixed amount for handling a legal matter regardless of the time spent or the difficulty of the tasks involved. Legal clinics and some lawyers charge flat rates for routine, uncontested matters such as name changes, simple wills and uncontested divorces.

Good cause   If a client fires an attorney for good cause, as defined by the state bar, the client may not be legally required to pay for all the attorney's services.

Grievance committee   See *Disciplinary agency*.

Hourly fee   Lawyer's fee based on the amount of time worked on a case. The fee is the hourly rate multiplied by the number of hours worked.

In pro per See *Pro se.*

Interrogatory Form of *discovery* in which written questions posed by one side in a lawsuit require written responses under oath by the other.

Judgment Final decision announced or written by a judge about the rights and claims of each side in a lawsuit.

Lawyer referral service Telephone service that provides the names and addresses of lawyers in a specific geographic area and by area of practice. Many are run by bar associations and charge a fee to the participating lawyers and law firms.

Legal malpractice Misconduct that, in the course of handling a case, harms a client. Most legal malpractice lawsuits are based on claims of *negligence* or *breach of contract.*

Mediation Informal alternative to suing in which both sides to a dispute meet with a neutral third party (mediator) to negotiate a resolution. The resolution is usually put into a written agreement that is signed by both sides.

Motion Request that a judge take specific action. (Example: a "motion to dismiss" is a request that the judge throw a case out of court.)

Negligence Legal doctrine on which a lawsuit is based, whereby the person being sued is accused of failing to do something that would normally be expected. Many *legal malpractice* cases are based on negligence.

Order Written command by a judge or court clerk describing a decision of the court, directing or forbidding an action, or issuing the final ruling of the court in a case.

Plaintiff Person who files a lawsuit against another.

Pleading Making a formal written statement of the claims or defenses of each side in a lawsuit.

Prepaid legal services Plan that provides legal services to members for a fixed monthly fee.

Pretrial conference Meeting of the lawyers and the judge, sometimes also including the parties to a lawsuit, to narrow the issues in the lawsuit, to agree on what will be presented at the trial and to make a final effort to settle the case without trial.

Pro se Representing yourself in court without the help of an attorney. Also called *in pro per.*

Proximate causation The direct connection between an event and the result that proves fault. In a *legal malpractice* case, the client must show that the attorney's misconduct or *negligence* was the "proximate cause" of the loss in order to recover money.

Reprimand   *Attorney discipline* whereby an attorney is either privately or publicly chastised for violating the state's *code of professional responsibility.* In both instances the lawyer is sent a letter explaining the misconduct and discipline. Also called *censure* or *admonition.*

Respondent   (1) The person against whom a *motion* is filed. (2) The person against whom an *appeal* is taken.

Retainer   Money asked by the lawyer before beginning work on a case, often considered a deposit for a portion of the work to be done. The money may be used to cover *expenses* or the lawyer's fee or simply to reserve the lawyer's services for a specified time period or lawsuit. The unused portion may or may not be refundable.

Ruling   A judge's decision on a legal question raised during a lawsuit.

Service   The delivery of a legal document by an officially authorized person to meet formal requirements of the applicable laws and assure that the person being sued is formally notified about the lawsuit or other legal action.

Settlement   An agreement about the final disposition of a lawsuit, including payment of debts, costs, and so forth.

Statute of limitations   A law that sets a time deadline for filing a lawsuit. This varies from state to state and with the basis of the lawsuit.

Subpoena   A court notice to compel the appearance of a witness or submission of documents or other evidence at a hearing; disobedience may be punishable as contempt of court.

Summons   (1) A notice delivered by a sheriff or other authorized person informing a *defendant* about a lawsuit. It notifies the defendant to appear in court at a specified time to respond to allegations in the lawsuit or risk losing the suit because of absence *(default judgment).* (2) A notice delivered by a sheriff or other authorized person informing someone to appear before a grand jury.

Summary judgment   A court's final decision based on the facts but issued before the end of a full trial.

Suspension   Discipline removing a lawyer's license to practice law in a specific state for a period of time ranging from a few days to several years for violating the *code of professional responsibility.*

Testimony   Oral or written evidence in the form of questions and answers given under oath.

Tort   A private wrong that causes injury to a person or property. Some *legal malpractice* cases are tort cases.

Withdrawal   An attorney's decision to stop working on a case and notification of the client about that decision.

BIBLIOGRAPHY

The following list includes books that deal with hiring and managing lawyers, books that discuss legal malpractice, and national directories of attorneys' names and addresses. The legal malpractice section includes the resources relied on most in our research but is by no means an exhaustive list of what is available. Check a law library or your public library's index for additional material. The books listed as out of print are available only in libraries.

Client-Attorney Relations

Competent Counsel: Working with Lawyers, by Denise G. Shekerjian. Dodd, Mead & Co., 6 Ram Ridge Rd., Spring Valley, NY 10977. 1985. $15.95. (Out of print.)
Advice on shopping for and managing a lawyer, legal costs, attorney discipline and legal malpractice cases. Also advice about alternatives to hiring a lawyer and complete list of state grievance committees.

Kill All the Lawyers? A Client's Guide to Hiring, Firing, Using and Suing Lawyers, by Sloan Bashinsky. Prentice-Hall, Gulf and Western Plaza, New York, NY 10023. 1986. $12.95. (Out of print.)
Anecdotes about lawyers, judges and clients. In sections with titles like "Greedy Lawyers," "Fee Generators" and "Clients Who Don't Pay," Bashinsky gives advice on what clients expect from lawyers, whether they can get it and at what cost.

The Lawyer Book: A Nuts and Bolts Guide to Client Survival, by Wesley J. Smith. Price/Stern/Sloan Publishers, 360 N. La Cienega Blvd., Los Angeles, CA 90048. 1987. $9.95.

In large print with many illustrations; shopping, managing and problem-solving techniques for maintaining healthy client-attorney relationship. Information on fee setting and on what legal tasks you can and cannot do on your own. Introduction by Ralph Nader.

One Hundred Ways To Cut Legal Fees & Manage Your Lawyer, by Erwin G. Krasnow and Robin S. Conrad. National Chamber Litigation Center, 1615 H St. NW, Washington, DC 20006. 1988. $10.95. Useful guide that presents lawyers as business people who need responsible, active management by their clients. Contains bibliography and list of federal statutes that authorize recovering attorneys' fees under certain circumstances.

Putting a Lid on Legal Fees: How to Deal Effectively with Lawyers, by Raymond M. Klein. Interlink Press, 908 Kenfield Ave., Los Angeles, CA 90049. 1986. $12.95. Intended for business clients; includes advice and information also useful to other clients. Basic advice: "Participate, don't abdicate." Covers shopping, hiring and managing a lawyer, with special emphasis on how fees are generated, what litigation can cost and how to keep down legal fees.

The Terrible Truth about Lawyers: How Lawyers Really Work & How to Deal with Them Successfully, by Mark H. McCormack. Beech Tree Books, William Morrow and Co., 105 Madison Ave., New York, NY 10016. 1987. $17.95. Written for business clients. Draws on author's experience as both lawyer and business client. Anecdotes and axioms illustrate points. Example: "They'll spend more of it, the less the client seems to care."

What Every Client Needs To Know About Using a Lawyer, by Gregory White Smith and Steven Naifeh. G. P. Putnam's Sons, 200 Madison Ave., New York, NY 10016. 1982. $13.95. (Out of print.) Comprehensive how-to book by two Harvard Law School graduates. Addresses clients' biggest fears—that lawyers are too expensive, dishonest or incompetent. Advice on shopping, managing and paying lawyers. Also good discussion of legal malpractice.

What Lawyers Do . . . And How to Make Them Work for You, by Daniel R. White. E. P. Dutton, 2 Park Ave., New York, NY 10016. 1987. $17.95. (Out of print.) Describes use and role of lawyers in most common legal situations, family law, taxes, estate planning, housing and death. Usu-

ally advises hiring lawyer, but does list alternatives like mediation and legal clinics.

*What You Aren't Supposed to Know about the Legal Profession—An
Exposé of Lawyers, Law Schools, Judges and More,* by Laurens
R. Schwartz. Shapolsky Publishers, 136 W. 22nd St., New York, NY
10011. 1988. $14.95.

Inside glimpse at why lawyers think and behave as they do.
Sometimes irreverent, always funny and revealing, pokes fun at
law school training, law firm antics and legal profession in general. Does not include systematic advice on hiring or working
with attorneys.

*Winning with Your Lawyer: What Every Client Should Know about
How the Legal System Works,* by Burton Marks and Gerald Gold-
farb. McGraw-Hill, 1221 Ave. of the Americas, New York, NY
10021. 1987 (2nd Ed.). $8.00. (Out of print.)

The first part offers tips on selecting and working with attorneys,
the second on how to manage attorneys in specific legal situations (personal injury, divorce, estate planning, crime and property rights).

Legal Malpractice Resources

American Jurisprudence, Second Edition, Vol. 7. (*Am. Jur.* 2d). The
Lawyers Cooperative Publishing Co., Aqueduct Bldg., Rochester,
NY 14694. 1980. See especially: "Liability of Attorneys for Mal-
practice," Sections 197–231. Available at law libraries.

Legal encyclopedia of general information about various types
of law and legal concepts. Written in plain English. Includes cross-
references and bibliographies of primary sources.

Corpus Juris Secundum, Vol. 7A. *(C.J.S.)* West Publishing Co., 50 W.
Kellogg Blvd., St. Paul, MN 55164. 1980. See especially: "Liability
for Negligence or Malpractice," Sections 255–276.

More comprehensive legal encyclopedia series than *Am. Jur.* but
written only for lawyers and harder to understand. General information about various types of law and legal concepts. Includes
case law citations.

*How to Sue Your Lawyer: The Consumer Guide to Legal Malprac-
tice,* by Hilton L. Stein. Legal Malpractice Institute, 103 Washington St., Morristown, NJ 07960. 1989. $19.95.

Step-by-step guide for filing legal malpractice case. Author calls
on personal experience to detail what goes on in typical malpractice case.

Lawyers' Manual on Professional Conduct. American Bar Association and Bureau of National Affairs, Inc. 1231 25th St. NW, Washington, DC 20037. See especially: Legal Malpractice, Section 301, pages 101–901. 1984. Available at library.

In plain English, 2,000-plus-page looseleaf book for lawyers who handle malpractice cases. Includes practical information on wide variety of topics, including legal malpractice, full text of ABA Model Rules of Professional Conduct and selected ABA ethics opinions from state and local bar associations.

Legal Malpractice, by Ronald E. Mallen and Jeffrey M. Smith. West Publishing Co., 50 W. Kellogg Blvd., St. Paul, MN 55164. 2 volumes. 1989 (3rd Ed.). $137.80.

In plain English, but intended for lawyers. Most comprehensive resource available on laws governing legal malpractice litigation. Includes exhaustive list of cases. Try to find it in public or local law library.

Modern Legal Ethics, by Charles W. Wolfram. West Publishing Co., 50 W. Kellogg Blvd., St. Paul, MN 55164. 1986 (1st Ed.). $28.95.

Broad, in-depth analysis of lawyer's responsibilities, written for law students. Theoretical summary of current law and discussion of possible future trends. Also summarizes current malpractice cases and related topics, lawyer and legal system regulation, professional discipline, client-attorney relationship, competence, etc.

Profile of Legal Malpractice: A Statistical Study of Determinative Characteristics of Claims Asserted Against Attorneys. Standing Committee on Lawyers' Professional Liability, American Bar Association, 750 N. Lake Shore Dr., Chicago, IL 60611. 1986. Free.

Statistical analysis of 29,227 malpractice claims against attorneys between 1983 and 1985. Graphs and charts present data about nature and size of legal malpractice complaints.

Lawyer Shopping Directories

The American Lawyer Guide to Leading Law Firms, by Steven Brill. AM-Law Publishing Co., New York, NY 10016. 2 volumes. 1983–84. (Out of print.)

An alphabetical list of 234 law firms by city. Each firm's entry is extensive, including the percentage of lawyers in the firm by specialty, names of some clients and law schools most of its attorneys attended. Lawyers and firms listed work in almost every area *except* legal malpractice.

The Best Lawyers in America, by Steven Naifeh and Gregory White
Smith. Putnam Publishing Group, 200 Madison Ave., New York,
NY 10016. 1984. (Out of print.)
Almost 200 lawyers listed by specialty. No biographical informa-
tion. Lawyers selected based on questionnaires completed by
2,000 lawyers.

Directory of the Legal Profession, by Ben Gerson. N.Y. Law Publishing Co., New York, NY 10016. 1984. (Out of print.)
More than 600 firms listed alphabetically by state and city. Entries
include listing by specialty such as litigation, labor, general business, corporate, real estate and entertainment/sports.

Lawyers' Register by Specialties and Fields of Law, by Margaret A.
Schultz. Lawyers' Register Publishing Company, 30700 Bain-
bridge Rd., Suite H, Solon, OH 44139. 1988 (9th Ed.). $99.50.
About 1,000 lawyers by specialty. Each entry includes lawyer's
name, address, specialization and, in some cases, biographical
note supplied by lawyer. Lawyers included are suggested by
ABA.

Martindale-Hubbell Law Directory. Martindale-Hubbell, 630 Central
Ave., New Providence, NJ 07974. 8 volumes. 1988. $195.
600,000 American and Canadian lawyers listed alphabetically by
state and by categories (U.S. government, international, patent
lawyers). Each entry has biography, including the lawyer's education, specialty, law firm, date of admittance to the bar and
"rating." Latter is of little practical value since it is based on
information supplied by fellow lawyers, not by clients.

Who's Who in American Law. Macmillan Directory Division, 3002
Glenview Rd., Wilmette, IL 60091. 1987–88 (5th Ed.). Approximately $165.
About 24,000 lawyers listed alphabetically, with biographical
notes. Finding lawyer in specific state or with specific expertise
requires browsing through entire directory. Lawyers selected by
assessing "incumbency in a defined position of responsibility" or
"attainment of a significant level of achievement."

About the Author

Kay Ostberg is the Deputy Director of HALT—An Organization of Americans for Legal Reform. She has contributed to HALT's library of educational materials as author of the *Directory of Lawyers Who Sue Lawyers* and the "Attorney Discipline National Survey and Report." Ms. Ostberg is a member of the National Federation of Paralegal Associations Advisory Board. She earned a J.D. in 1983 from the National Law Center at George Washington University and also holds a B.A., cum laude, from Columbia University's Barnard College. She is also a coauthor of *Everyday Contracts.*